S0-DUU-526

Automated Library Circulation Systems, 1979-80

2nd edition

by Alice Harrison Bahr

Knowledge Industry Publications, Inc.
White Plains, New York 10604

Professional Librarian Series

Automated Library Circulation Systems, 1979-80
by Alice Harrison Bahr

Library of Congress Cataloging in Publication Data

Bahr, Alice Harrison
   Automated library circulation systems, 1979-80.

   (Professional librarian series)
   First ed. (1977) by P. Dranov.
   Bibliography: p.
   Includes index.
   1. Libraries — Circulation, loans — Data processing.
I. Dranov, Paula.   Automated library circulation
systems, 1977-78.   II. Title.   III.   Series.
Z712.D7   1979   025.6'028'54   79-16189
ISBN 0-914236-34-2

Printed in the United States of America

Copyright © 1979 by Knowledge Industry Publications, Inc., 2 Corporate Park Drive, White Plains, N.Y. 10604. Not to be reproduced in any form whatever without written permission from the publisher.

LIBRARY
LOS ANGELES COUNTY MUSEUM OF NATURAL HISTORY

Contents

I. Introduction 1

II. An Overview of Automated Circulation Systems 5

III. Criteria for System Acquisition 18

IV. The Market Today: Available Systems 24

    Checkpoint/Plessey 24

    CLASSIC 29

    LIBS 100 (CLSI) 36

    DataPhase 46

    Decicom 51

    Gaylord 53

    SCICON 61

    ULISYS 66

    ICC/Plessey 70

    Innovated Systems 71

    Knogo 72

    CIRC 72

V. Users' Comments 74

VI. Implications of Automated Circulation 79

VII. Conclusions 84

Appendix: Directory of Manufacturers Offering and Libraries
      Using Automated Systems 87

Bibliography 101

Index 103

About the Author 105

Figures and Illustrations

Checkpoint/Plessey flush mounted 1130 terminal 26
Checkpoint/Plessey portable terminal 27
JRL-1000 light pen 31
Cincinnati Electronics microcomputer 32
LIBS 100 laser scanner 38
LIBS 100 browsing terminal 39
Figure IV-1. The Inquiry Process for a Search for
    Titles by a Given Author 42
Figure IV-2. Report Arranged by Classification
    Number and Patron Age 43
Figure IV-3. Report Arranged by Branch and Patron
    Status 43
Keypunch card conversion with LIBS 100 equipment 44
Data General keyboard, light pen scanner and CRT
    output screen 47
ECLIPSE S/100 hardware 48
Gaylord System's keyboard and light pen terminal
    with CRT display 55
Figure IV-4. Example of Report Generated by Gaylord
    Circulation System 59
SCICON checkout process 60

I

Introduction

According to Barbara Evans Markuson, circulation control will be "the major automation growth area during the next five years."[1] Full-capacity attendance at two December 1977 American Library Association institutes on "Automated Circulation Systems" (at both, an overflow of registrants was turned away) supports that prediction. In part, the growing interest may be attributed to technological advances which have increased competition and lowered costs.

The first full report on automated library circulation control systems appeared in the July and September issues of *Library Technology Reports* in 1975. When it was updated in May 1977, only one of the originally described systems was still available; and four new vendors had entered the market. By early 1979 the picture had changed again, and drastically. Not only had one vendor withdrawn from the marketplace, but three more had entered and even more stood on the sidelines, planning to enter at some future time.

Vendors with installed, operative systems and those awarded contract bids in 1978 were:

- Checkpoint/Plessey
- Cincinnati Electronics (CLASSIC)
- C L Systems, Inc.
- DataPhase
- Decicom Systems, Inc. (abandoned the market in 1979)
- Gaylord Bros., Inc.
- Systems Control, Inc. (SCICON)
- Universal Library Systems, Inc. (ULISYS)

---

[1] Barbara Evans Markuson, "Granting Amnesty and Other Aspects of Automated Circulation," *American Libraries,* April 1978, p. 205.

Planning to enter the market after successful system implementation are Knogo Corporation, in conjunction with the British firm Automated Library Systems, Ltd., and the University of Toronto Library Automation System, a network serving 46 Canadian libraries which is currently installing its system, referred to as CIRC, in the University of Toronto undergraduate library.

Other institutions with home-grown systems (systems designed by libraries around commercially available equipment) plan to enter the market at less specified times. For instance, the East Brunswick (N.J.) Public Library, whose on-line system was designed by city data processing staff, is presently accepting bids from vendors who may wish to market the system. Bucknell University (Lewisburg, Pa.) still uses an off-line system it developed (BLOCS I) which relies on punched cards for data input. However, BLOCS II, an on-line system which uses bar-coded labels to input data, is currently under development.* Honeywell, which supplies the system's computer, may market the system at some future time.

The increased market activity is good for libraries. Struggling for economic survival, vendors have become more responsive to the library's needs. As a consequence, newer systems are more flexible. One example of that flexibility is the trend either to sell software separately or to design it so that libraries may modify programs. Partly as a result of increased competition, optical character recognition (OCR) is now a standard option in many systems. Reserve book modules are available, as are a greater number of conversion methods.

The greatest boost to the competition responsible for the development of new features is a series of hardware innovations: the minicomputer, the microcomputer and the 1647 series of terminals from Epic Data. It's difficult to define terms like mini and microcomputer since their capabilities change almost daily. However, the mini was once what the microcomputer now is: a small machine dedicated to a single purpose, limited in the amount of storage and in the amount and kind of software that it can accommodate. Introduced in the early 1970s, the minicomputer made it possible for libraries to have stand-alone systems (systems relying on a computer housed in the library). Today, because of more sophisticated software, minis can store as much as four million bytes of core storage and some can support well over 30 on-line circulation terminals. The future may hold the same promise for microcomputers, currently dedicated to small off-line systems.

Initially, terms like mini and micro designated less capability. However, they also referred to size. For example, Bill Scholtz points out in the May 1977 issue of *Library Technology Reports* that in 1960 the IBM 1620 computer occupied a 20 x 30 foot room; by 1974, a machine capable of the same tasks occupied nine square feet and could be carried from room to room. In 1971, when the first one-chip central processing unit

---

* For a full description of BLOCS I, consult ERIC documents ED 09 46 97 and ED 09 46 98. For information on BLOCS I and II, contact Ms. Helena Rivoire, Chief of Technical Services at Bucknell University Library.

was revealed, it took up an area of about a sixth of an inch long and an eighth of an inch wide. "Yet this inert microprocessor had a calculating capacity almost equal to the room-size ENIAC — the first fully electronic computer, completed in 1946."[2] Today, the minis and micros do more than save space; they rival the capabilities of larger units.

The Epic Data terminals, model series 1647, have facilitated conversion for libraries relying on keypunched book cards for circulation. Terminals may be modified to reformat and transfer data from 80-column punch cards to an on-line disk storage medium.

Technological strides like these reduce costs, and reduced costs are a significant part of librarians' renewed interest in automated circulation control systems. Markuson indicates that in 1963 hardware alone for a proposed circulation control system for the Library of Congress was estimated at $1 million. Today, hardware and software could be supplied for one third that cost.[3] Ken Sheedy, vice president of Universal Library Systems, Inc., believes that the system installed at the Phoenix Public Library in 1977 for $350,000 could be installed today for approximately $220,000. A number of newly developed off-line and on-line microcomputer based absence systems designed for small libraries range in price from $10,000 to $30,000.

While increased competition and price reductions make a more attractive market, they do not minimize the complexity of the decision process. Only a dedicated examination of what competing systems offer, a thorough study of how those systems operate and a sure grasp of the library's future development, i.e., the uses to which a machine-readable data base will be put, assure a reasonable choice. To assist in that painstaking task, this report reviews present systems' capabilities, design and performance, defines key terms, outlines important selection questions and discusses implications of automated library circulation control systems. Based on independent research, evaluation of vendor-supplied information and informal user interviews, the study reaches the following conclusions:

- The trend away from punched book cards and embossed IDs to on-line minicomputer based systems continues to accelerate.

- The low cost of microprocessors is stimulating the development and marketing of off-line circulation systems for small libraries.

- Flexible system design, maximizing the library's options, is emphasized in the newer systems.

- While many libraries employ several automated systems autonomously, several are making circulation the hub of automated processes, using circulation terminals to interact with other data bases.

---

2 "The Age of Miracle Chips," *Time,* 111:44 (February 20, 1978).

3 Markuson, "Granting Amnesty," p. 207.

• Most users have not had sufficient time to exploit all the potential of their circulation systems.

• The emphasis on networking will continue to stimulate interest in automated library circulation control systems.

• While home-grown systems continue to be developed and to influence the market, a number of libraries initially using them have switched to packaged systems.

• The main impetus for automation of circulation remains the desire to provide better service and maintain better control over the collection.

II

An Overview
of Automated Circulation Systems

In 1977 Dranov provided an excellent survey of the automated circulation control system's development. She traced its origin from the in-house developed, off-line system (one designed to capture, store and later print out data about materials out of the library in circulation) developed by universities and municipal data processing departments in the early 1960s to the on-line, minicomputer-based inventory control systems. These were made possible in the 1970s by the simultaneous development of both minicomputers and light pens able to read and transmit data from bar-coded labels to a minicomputer.[1] Documenting transitions, Dranov indicated that the University of South Carolina's McKissick Library was the first to use light pens for circulation and that the first packaged, commercially available system was (and still is) offered by C L Systems, Inc. (CLSI) in Newtonville, Mass.

Building on that history, this chapter will clarify the terminology and the issues involved in the automation of circulation: terms like home-grown, packaged, absence, inventory, off-line, on-line and issues like call number vs. access number, OCR labels vs. bar-coded labels, conversion, electronic security system interface and cost. Preceding that, however, is a synopsis of why libraries have and have not automated.

In 1975 Butler estimated that 800 libraries were involved in some automated procedures.[2] Small as that figure is and despite some libraries' increasing transaction figures,

---

[1] Paula Dranov, *Automated Library Circulation Systems, 1977-1978* (White Plains, NY: Knowledge Industry Publications, Inc., 1977), pp. 13-15.

[2] "Butler Says 800 Libraries Involved in Automation," *Advanced Technology/Libraries* (October 1975), p. 10.

less than half that number now have automated circulation processes. Why? The slow response is a matter of cost, expertise and size. Unless the library is joining a circulation network, average costs for an on-line system are about $100,000. Few libraries can afford that outlay unless they can demonstrate the system's cost effectiveness, are awarded a grant or special funding or are faced with major equipment replacement. Even those with funds often prefer to live with the system they know rather than combat the less known exigencies of the computer. Lastly, one rule of thumb is that transactions under 200,000 a year may be handled manually without great difficulty. For some, the manual and photographic systems perform well enough and at a reasonable cost.

For libraries with annual transactions exceeding 200,000, the limitations of the typical manual or semi-automatic systems become increasingly evident. Except for batch processing systems, preparation of overdue notices is a time-consuming and troublesome task. In manual and photographic systems, files must be searched manually and notices either typed or written out. One reason the University of Pennsylvania's Van Pelt Library switched from an IBM System 7 to CLSI was that the off-line batch-processing system afforded no control over fines after first notices were generated.

Another time-consuming manual task is filing. In 1977 the Commack (N.Y.) Public Library circulated 267,640 items. On a particularly busy day when 1200 items circulated, the staff knew that half of the next day would be devoted to filing. Usually four people were needed to file the previous day's book cards, which were separated into a number of categories. For example, children's fiction was separated from children's nonfiction. Now, using Gaylord's Automated Library Circulation Control System, the library's filing is eliminated and overdue notices are mailed within 10 days rather than after two or three months.

Photographic systems eliminate the necessity of filing, but like the manual systems they pose serious collection control problems. Until book cards are sorted and filed and microfilm records of transactions are developed, the staff cannot determine whether a book is out. The process is even more difficult with microfilmed transactions since they are recorded as they occur, not in call number order. Off-line systems, like manual card file systems, involve a time lag between checkouts and available library records. Moreover, placing a reserve on an item in any of those systems is a difficult, unwieldy task.

In addition, there are a number of tasks that manual and semi-automatic systems do not perform. None calculates fines automatically, records borrower statistics, places reserves automatically, catches delinquent borrowers or handles inquiries about the status of a particular item.

Traditionally, then, libraries turn to automation to reduce time-consuming clerical routines, to provide better service, new services and greater control over the collection. A few can justify automation on a cost-containment basis alone. For example, the Greensboro (N.C.) Public Library determined that an automated circulation system would reduce staff by three or four full-time persons, an annual saving of between $40,000 and $45,000. When the Tucson (Ariz.) Public Library's 15-year-old, outdated Regiscope equipment deteriorated, the library discovered that an automated circulation package was not much more costly than comparable equipment replacement. Similarly, when the Dallas (Texas) Community College District decided to open three new campuses, it faced the option of purchasing expensive semi-automatic equipment, Standard Register equipment to take IBM punched cards, or an on-line package; again, the cost differential among them was insignificant.

New buildings open up new possibilities. Just as the Dallas Community College District switched to DataPhase when opening its new campuses, the Northland Public Library (Pittsburgh, Pa.) commemorated its 10th anniversary with a new building and a ULISYS automated circulation control system. Purchased to offset a growing circulation rate in a new building with multiple exits, ULISYS has become the lever for automating other functions in the library. Laura Shelley, library director, now plans to contact BALLOTS for cataloging, and Baker & Taylor and Brodart for acquisitions. Moreover, she hopes to convince local school libraries to purchase terminals to make inquiries of the public library's data base, thereby facilitating interlibrary loan requests. A final reason for automating circulation, then, is to provide a hub or nucleus for further automation and to tie together community resources.

IN-HOUSE DEVELOPED SYSTEMS

In-house or home-grown systems, those designed by libraries around commercially available equipment, were the first automated circulation systems. Usually they relied on punched book cards being read at circulation terminals which stored patron ID, book ID and due date for transferral to a host main computer. Whether at a university, municipal or commercial data processing center, host facilities use the collected information to produce printouts of checked out materials, usually arranged by call number. Frequency of printouts is determined by the library and sometimes by the center's own workloads and priorities. Typically, printouts are issued daily, semi-weekly or weekly.

The capabilities of such systems vary, and the early systems became prototypes for later ones. For instance, a few early systems had some on-line capabilities. Today Checkpoint/Plessey offers an off-line system with optional on-line book status. In other words, printouts continue to be generated on a predetermined basis; however, should the library need to know the status of a book immediately, it may do so. Similarly, host facilities of many early systems prepared overdue notices at specified intervals. This is the distributed processing concept behind Gaylord Bros.' current automated library circulation control system. While all borrower and staff transactions are recorded immediately, they are transferred nightly to the host computer, which prepares all notices.

The impetus for a library to design its own system seems to be fourfold:

- No other acceptable systems are available.
- Knowledgeable data processing staff are available.
- There is a need for greater flexibility than available systems offer.
- Self-design appears to be less expensive.

In the late 1960s the University of Pittsburgh designed an off-line, batch-processing system relying on an IBM 11/30. Transactions were processed every three or four days. Pittsburgh had little other choice: No commercial, packaged systems were then available. In the early 1970s both Bucknell University and Syracuse University developed their own off-line systems for the same reason. With time, all have made major modifications in hardware and software, some quite costly. At present, all are planning some future on-line capabilities.

Another reason universities design their own systems is that most have computer equipment and staff already available to them. For example, the library circulation system developed in the late 1960s at Ohio State University by library and IBM staff ran on the university's IBM 360/50 computer system. Now called the Library Control System, LCS has been transplanted to the State University of New York (SUNY) at Albany and the University of Illinois.

However, even though a plethora of commercial systems are currently available, home-grown systems continue to be developed, whether for independence or because they are cost effective. For some it is both. The East Brunswick (N.J.) Public Library was fortunate in two respects. First, the township's data processing center is next door, providing unusually convenient expertise and service. Second, the township did not bill the library for its programming time, which was the equivalent of one man-year. As a consequence, the library's on-line inventory system, which includes three IBM 3277 CRTs and two Recognition Products, Inc. Model P130 OCR wands tied to an IBM 3/15 at the data processing center, cost only $28,000 to develop. The least expensive, comparable packaged system was approximately $100,000. Therefore, even if programming time were assessed at $40,000, the library saved money.

The same was true for the Macon/Bibb County (Ga.) Public Library. Modeled after a system developed for the Oklahoma City Library, the Macon/Bibb County Public Library's automated light pen system, comprised of IBM and NCR hardware and Monarch bar-coded labels and wands, cost only $18,000 to install in the main library and in four branches.[3]

In addition to potential cost effectiveness, however, there are still other reasons for designing a system in-house. As East Brunswick library director Edward Whittaker explains, "The system devised for the East Brunswick Public Library gives us greater flexibility and allows us to cull from the system exactly what we want." As an example, the library is currently pulling out all circulation statistics for the past two years by location code (adult, etc.) and by Dewey classification number. This information, providing a profile of patron reading habits, is an effective tool for collection and special program development.

The impact of custom in-house systems on automated library circulation can be phenomenal. For example, the University of Chicago Library-designed terminal, the

---

[3] " 'Home Brew' Saves Money in Georgia," *Library Journal* (March 15, 1977), p. 673.

JRL-1000, was the beginning of Cincinnati Electronics' on-line circulation system, CLASSIC.

Although sometimes cost-effective and usually more flexible, custom systems have not always proven more desirable than the commercial packaged systems. At least one large university currently using an off-line system it developed would eagerly purchase a packaged system if funds were available. This would give the library greater control over its operations. Independent of the university's computer center, the library could set its own priorities instead of having them established by the university. American University (Washington, D.C.) and the University of Pennsylvania switched from their own systems to CLSI. The ultimate value of self-design is determined largely by environment. If hardware and programming expertise are available, relatively inexpensive and capable of meeting library specifications, the home-grown system is a viable alternative to the packaged system.

PACKAGED SYSTEMS

Packaged systems, those designed by commercial vendors who offer hardware, software and often maintenance in one total systems package, free the library both from choosing hardware and from programming, which is often more expensive than equipment outlay. These systems are referred to as turnkey systems; presumably the librarian merely turns a key to activate the entire system. While that is a simplification, the packaged system's drawing card is that the vendor, not the library, is responsible for system development and maintenance. Ironically, as time goes on, libraries are becoming increasingly interested in controlling the computers that control their operations; hence, a number of vendors now allow libraries to maintain their own software and thereby to modify and enhance programs.

Vendors

The first available packaged system was introduced by C L Systems, Inc. (then called Computer Library Services) in 1973. Since then 12 other vendors have entered the market. Many more are planning to join them, but there has also been an exodus of some who have not met with the success they had sought.

One of the 12, Check-a-Book, sold its on-line minicomputer-based system to 3M Co. in 1975. In February 1978 3M Co. announced that its Inventory Control System (ICS), already installed at the Arlington County (Va.) Public Libraries and at Princeton University, would be withdrawn. A second vendor, IBM, withdrew software support for its System/7 computer after assisting in development at the University of Pennsylvania. Although several libraries continue to use IBM hardware for custom designed systems, the University of Pennsylvania eventually adopted CLSI. A third vendor, Mohawk Data recently announced that it was not accepting new customers for its 4400 system, a batch-processing system relying on punched cards. A fourth company multiplied rather than reduced the number of vendors on the market. Plessey Telecommunications, an English concern, markets its three off-line and partially on-line systems through Checkpoint Systems, Inc. and its fourth, totally on-line system, through International Computing.

LOS ANGELES COUNTY MUSEUM OF NATURAL HISTORY

At present, then, eight vendors are marketing four different types of automated circulation control systems:

1)   Off-line batch processing systems relying on host computers to generate circulation printouts (Checkpoint/Plessey).

2)   Off-line batch processing systems with optional on-line book status inquiry (Checkpoint/Plessey).

3)   Distributed processing systems in which all local functions are on-line, but certain tasks like issue of overdue notices are handled by a host computer (Gaylord).

4)   Stand-alone, on-line systems (C L Systems, Cincinnati Electronics, DataPhase, ICC/Plessey, Systems Control and Universal Library Systems).

ABSENCE SYSTEMS

Most libraries with a manual book card or photographic charging system already have an absence circulation system, one which records only those items checked out of the library. Absence literally means absent from the library. With such systems, full bibliographic records of checked-out items need not be kept. Enough information must be recorded to permit access to the library's full bibliographic record of its holdings, the shelflist. Usually that means call number. However, author and brief title provide a double check on records' accuracy and permit staff and patron alike another access route to the shelflist (i.e., in the case of lost but not overdue books when the patron does not know the call numbers). Because a great amount of data need not be stored, automated circulation systems which work around the absence design require less storage space and are consequently less expensive than those working around the inventory design.

Librarians seem to want more and be willing to pay for more today. None of the systems described in this report are absence systems, which effectively constitute the first step in automated circulation control. What absence systems eliminate is the manual drudgery of filing and preparing overdues. For some, that is all that automation is required to do and a number of in-house systems continue to operate in the absence mode.

Such systems speed up traditional circulation routines, but hardly redefine the department's role. Instead of patrons having to wait while a librarian culls endless card files to locate a book, an irrevocable black and white printout has an immediate and definite result. Inventory systems, on the other hand, can alter the nature and function of the circulation department, making it the hub of most library activities.

INVENTORY SYSTEMS

Like absence systems, inventory systems require that at least the library's circulating materials be identified in machine-readable form. While some rely on punched cards, as do most absence systems, the majority rely on bar-coded labels — unique machine-readable numeric identifiers providing access to more complete bibliographic files stored in the computer's data base of holdings. The main distinction between an absence system and an inventory system is that an inventory system maintains a permanent file of all holdings converted to machine-readable form.

What that means to the library depends on how complete holding files are, what kind of access is provided to them and how the library plans to employ such information. For instance, the Northland Public Library near Pittsburgh decided to include subject heading references in its data base of holdings. Its Universal Library System, Inc. circulation control system (ULISYS) is totally on-line. Therefore, some reference responsibilities may be partially assumed by circulation attendants. The degree to which automation affects the library's organizational structure is determined by the library. What inventory systems mean technically is that a larger computer is needed; what they mean managerially is that a greater variety of statistical and managerial reports are available.

OFF-LINE VS. ON-LINE

While absence and inventory refer to how much information about the library's collection should be recorded and how long it should be maintained, on-line and off-line refer to how that information is accessed. The majority of currently available systems are on-line and real time; that is, as transactions are recorded, files are instantly updated and the most current information is immediately available to library staff. In off-line or batch-processing systems, information is stored or captured at terminals and processed by a central computer at a later time. It cannot be directly accessed by staff. Simply stated, the off-line system records data, but does not interact with it. The on-line system, which, for example, has been directed to trap delinquent borrowers and catch overdue books that are on reserve, is forced to interact with all new data. Because it is asked to do more, it demands more from the library: a larger computer and more equipment, such as video display terminals and random access storage.

While most systems are advertised as totally on-line, that is a misnomer. It is more correct to think of functions rather than systems as on-line. For instance, the Gaylord Bros. system places files of delinquent borrowers, certain statistical reports and item status on-line. Library staff can identify all delinquent borrowers listed in the file and may query the data base for an item's status at any time and receive the most current information. However, a patron who becomes delinquent on a particular day is not in the on-line file until the following day when the host computer updates the delinquent borrowers' file. In most other systems, some functions are off-line, usually detailed reports.

ACCESS NUMBER VS. CALL NUMBER

For several reasons, most automated systems require that circulating materials or materials incorporated in a permanent data base be identified by a unique numeric designation rather than by a call number. In academic libraries, call numbers are often complex or too long to fit the allowed character space and too prone to error when keyed in manually. In public libraries, call numbers often do not uniquely identify an item. To assure that every item may be identified uniquely, each is assigned an access number.

There are several advantages to unique numeric designators. Since only numbers need be entered, additional keyboarding is unnecessary. A simple number keyboard, less expensive than a full keyboard unit, can handle transactions. Moreover, such access numbers allow the library to circulate materials prior to cataloging, especially when pre-punched cards and sequential machine-readable labels are available from vendors. Preparing either in-house would be costly.

For those libraries that still find call number access useful, some vendors do make such systems available: CLSI, Cincinnati Electronics, ICC/Plessey, Systems Control and Universal Library Systems.

OCR LABELS VS. BAR-CODED LABELS

Most automated systems use bar-coded labels to identify both patrons and items. In several systems, however, OCR (optical character recognition) labels are an option: CLSI, DataPhase, Systems Control and Universal Library Systems. Both are in common use today. Bar codes are found on most food products and magazines today, while OCR numbers are on the bottom of bank checks. Both serve the same purpose: They uniquely identify an item or person in a form that the computer can translate into its own language.

While some vendors (who have incorporated bar codes) are not sure that OCR technology has proven itself, libraries choosing such labels accrue certain benefits. For one, they are cheaper than bar codes, whose production must conform to more rigid technical requirements. Second, unlike bar-coded labels, they may be produced in-house using a typewriter (such as an IBM Selectric) with an OCR font. On the negative side, OCR labels smudge more easily than bar-coded labels, which are produced by a photographic process. In some instances, the OCR wand requires a steadier hand than does the bar code reading light pen to get a successful read.

CONVERTING TO AUTOMATION

Those who have undergone the traumas of bringing an automated system into operation would likely agree with one library director: "Conversion does not go as smoothly as any vendor tells you it will." It would be surprising to hear the contrary, since years of effort go into the construction of a library's bibliographic records. Converting even a shortened version of those to machine-readable form is a monumental undertaking requiring great forethought. Even with 25 employees paid under the Comprehensive Employment and Training Act (CETA) and working 13 hours a week, six hours a day on 20 terminals, the Tacoma Public Library anticipates that it will take a full year to convert its 500,000 volumes.

Like automation itself, conversion techniques have evolved. Initially, conversion meant keypunching cards based on shelflist information and then transferring the data to tape. The amount of information recorded depended on available field space and on the uses to which the data base would be put. Costs were estimated to be $1.50 or $1.60 per title.[4] Prior to going on-line in September 1977, the Manhattan (Kan.) Public Library, which uses the Gaylord System, converted its 100,000 titles in this manner.

Today, more common than the error-prone keypunching approach is the matching of library holdings against another library's holdings which are already in machine-readable form. And sometimes, data bases are supplied by vendors. For example, Systems Control, Inc. provides a data base of 300,000 titles as part of its circulation control system package. C L Systems will assist the library to develop a holdings profile and then search for a compatible data base. Oftentimes, however, that is the library's responsibility. When the Tacoma Public Library went on-line in April 1978 with DataPhase System, it purchased Blackwell North America, Inc.'s tape data base of 1.9 million titles. Tacoma estimates that 80% of its titles could be matched to the Blackwell base, which has been stripped to an abbreviated record so that it could be entered into Tacoma's minicomputer.[5]

For titles not matching entries in another library's data base, the usual approach is to key data in manually via circulation terminals; only Checkpoint/Plessey I does not permit the data base to be built this way. Some libraries select manual keying as the sole conversion technique. When the Phoenix Public Library purchased a Universal Library Systems, Inc. on-line circulation control system, it keyed in its 1 million volumes. The task was somewhat easier for the Northland Public Library. Installing its ULISYS system in October 1978 entailed keying in only 70,000 titles. Of course, few libraries keying data in manually have a complete data base before going on-line. Typically, a number of books will be converted while in circulation: bar-coded labels are affixed when an item circulates; when it is returned, it is flagged by the terminal for full data entry. Tacoma's director, Kevin Hagerty, estimates that manual keying takes "10 times as long" as matching titles.[6] Regardless of how the title base is constructed, however, some manual keying is inevitable when data specific to the library is entered.

For libraries with data already in machine-readable form, there are three options. Keypunched cards can be transferred to tape by the vendor or a service bureau. Keypunched cards may also be used to transfer data directly to the library's disk storage file during checkout with the help of a special terminal manufactured by Epic Data and distributed by CL Systems. Called a Circulation/Conversion Station, it is used by both the University of Pennsylvania and American University. Finally, if the library's data base is already on tape, a number of vendors will reformat data to make it compatible with their systems.

Thanks to an innovative San Jose Public Library employee, OCLC members may now simultaneously enter circulation code numbers while cataloging new acquisitions.

---

4 "Library Saves $370,000 on System Conversion," *Computerworld* (May 1, 1978), p. 19.

5 Ibid.

6 Ibid.

The unit which makes that possible reads both OCR and bar-coded labels and is currently available from TPS Electronics. DataPhase also has an OCLC interface under development that would allow information on OCLC screens to be transferred to circulation terminals and entered in the circulation system data base.

While the future is bound to afford even more innovation and greater expertise in developing and refining conversion techniques, librarians should keep two things in mind. First, while vendors assume varying degrees of responsibility for conversion, the ultimate burden falls to the library. Automated circulation is still too new for many vendors to have had complete experience with all conversion techniques in a variety of different environments. A few libraries which converted early and allowed vendors to convert their shelflists for them were not totally satisfied with the end result. Consequently, many libraries' specifications detail the conversion technique they wish to use.

Second, one reason for dissatisfaction with vendor-controlled shelflist keypunching was inadequate shelflist preparation. If the shelflist has been variously marked and coded over the years, detailed explanations regarding what is to be entered must be compiled. If only brief data will be recorded, the library must realize that such an abbreviated data base would not be serviceable for any future on-line cataloging plans. Automating circulation provides a good excuse for taking inventory. A few smaller libraries now regret not having taken inventory prior to converting; larger institutions appear more willing to live with a few errors.

ELECTRONIC SECURITY SYSTEM CONNECTIONS

There is little, if any, difficulty in having electronic security systems located close to automated library circulation control systems. The Commack (N.Y.) Public Library has Gaylord Book Theft Detection System screens three feet from its Gaylord Circulation Control System terminals and has experienced no difficulties with interference. The San Jose Public Library employs the 3M Tattle-Tape Detection System in conjunction with a Systems Control, Inc. circulation system (SCICON) and reports no problems.

However, a few libraries did have problems with their electronic security systems when their circulation systems were first installed. For instance, the Dallas Community College District reported an initial problem with Tattle-Tape screens and DataPhase CRTs. The Biomedical Library at UCLA had similar difficulties with Tattle-Tape screens and CLSI CRTs. In no case was the problem prolonged, nor was data recorded via circulation terminals hampered.[7] Radiation emitted from CRTs (placed too close to detection equip-

---

[7] A number of automated circulation systems have been integrated with electronic security systems. For example, the Innovated Systems circulation system at the University of Texas at Dallas is combined with the 3M Tattle-Tape Book Theft Detection System. Cincinnati Electronics' circulation system (CLASSIC) provides a connection with the Checkpoint/Mark II Book Theft Detection System, and other system combinations are being developed. Finally, the Knogo/ALS circulation system will be compatible with the Knogo Book Theft Detection System.

ment) interfered with detection equipment operation; in some cases, sensitized materials failed to signal alarms. The solution was a simple one: moving detection screens farther away from CRTs.

COST

Cost effectiveness of automated circulation systems is only one reason for their attractiveness. Some libraries, however, do report impressive savings. For example, the San Jose Public Library anticipates paying for its $465,600 Systems Control system within three years, based on the 17 employees it expects to eliminate through attrition. The Dallas Community College District and the Northland Public Library estimate that their systems will pay for themselves in about five years. According to Markuson, these payback results are about the best that can be hoped for. "If a system is at the *current* state of the art, is readily expandable in terms of added storage and terminals, and is cost-effective over a five to seven year period, that is about all the certainty one can expect in this uncertain world."[8]

For the most part, however, libraries are at least as interested in improving services as in realizing savings. In the early 1970s when IBM helped develop the Library Circulation System at Ohio State University, A. Robert Thorson, head of OSU's circulation department, defended development and maintenance costs of the home-grown system primarily on the basis of improved services. Although development and maintenance were each in the neighborhood of $400,000 (the latter continuing on an annual basis), Thorson acknowledged: "It was known that costs would exceed those incurred under a manual system but given the climate prevalent in the late 1960s, the automation of circulation functions appeared to be inevitable."[9]

With so little emphasis on cost, it's not surprising that so few cost benefit analyses have been done. Only one recent study has pinpointed costs for a particular type of system: shared time. At the Suburban Library System in Burr Ridge, Ill., 13 member libraries are linked together in a network by four C L Systems LIBS 100 systems. Members pay $750 a month for the first five years and $280 a month thereafter.[10] Rates are based on each library having one light pen terminal and one CRT terminal.

It is difficult to determine what, if any, dollar savings are realized by a library's use of an automated circulation system. A year ago, member libraries using manual systems discovered that the cost of circulating an individual item was between $.23 and

---

[8] Barbara Evans Markuson, "Granting Amnesty and Other Aspects of Automated Circulation," *American Libraries* (April 1978), p. 207.

[9] A. Robert Thorson, "The Economics of Automated Circulation," in *The Economics of Library Automation*, ed. J.L. Divilbiss (Clinic on Library Applications of Data Processing, 13th, University of Illinois, 1976), p. 40.

[10] "Online Circulation: Costs Pegged," *Library Journal* (April 15, 1977), p. 867.

$.35. Cost variation was partly due to who manned the circulation desk; in small libraries, in which professional librarians staffed the desk, costs accelerated. While the study was not conducted uniformly, each library measured different items to arrive at its calculation. The agreed-upon average cost to circulate one item was $.26.

One not-yet automated library in the system, the Blue Island Public Library, circulated 118,392 items in fiscal year 1978. At $.26 an item, total circulation costs for that year were $30,781.92. A comparable system library, the Harvey Public Library, circulated 105,892 items in the same fiscal year. At $750 a month, the cost of their automated circulation system, annual circulation costs were $9,000. That figure, however, is exclusive of staff salaries. At Harvey, that includes two full-time clerks, two part-time clerks and a head of circulation. Although it is unlikely that those salaries total less than $21,000, Donna Sundstrom, head librarian at Harvey, says, "I'd never go back to stamping, regardless of price."

Most libraries are content to gauge savings roughly. For example, one CLSI user, the Lewis and Clark Library (Helena, Mont.), increased circulation 80% with no additional staff. A second CLSI user, New York University, handled a 243% circulation increase one year after the system was operational.

Moreover, estimates often overlook a number of expenses not included in either purchase or service costs. Accordingly, potential purchasers should keep an eye on:

- Telecommunications costs: the continual telephone line changes to the distant network computer or among library branches or from mini to main computer.

- Conversion costs: the one-time expense of getting on the system.

- Supply costs (labels): small but ongoing.

- Site preparation costs: one time, but may be substantial for some facilities.

- Upgrading costs: adding capacity to meet new demands of growth in branches or transactions.

- Additional programming costs: to add features not included by the vendor.

SUMMARY

Both the market and technology for automated circulation control systems play integral roles in the on-going change characterizing the field. The first systems, mostly off-line absence systems, were developed in the early 1960s. In-house developed systems (ones designed by libraries around commercially available equipment) were usually designed by large universities or by municipal data processing staff which had technical expertise readily available. They were responding to manual systems which became increasingly cumbersome and costly to operate when transactions reached 200,000 annually. The early systems eliminated the time-consuming chores of filing cards and preparing overdue notices.

In the mid 1960s the minicomputer arrived, but only in the 1970s were packaged systems (ones developed commercially offering hardware, software and maintenance from one vendor) made available. Such on-line inventory systems, permitting direct access to a data base of the library's total holdings, did more than eliminate clerical routines: They provided greater collection control and new services. Patron receipts, bibliographies, and other notices could be printed, as could a greater variety of statistical and managerial reports. Delinquent borrowers could be trapped and the fines they incurred could be computed automatically. Data base inquiries to determine book and patron status could be made, and messages could be sent from one library to another via the systems' visual display units. While minimum costs for such systems are approximately $100,000, many librarians feel the qualitative service they make possible offsets both their initial outlay and on-going operating costs.

In the future, microcomputers will make available even more less costly alternatives. The present eight vendors offer everything from off-line inventory systems, some with certain on-line capabilities, to stand-alone systems. In the developmental stage, however, are on-line microprocessor-based absence systems for $10,000 or less. Eventually, the microprocessor-based systems will rival the capacity of present minicomputers. Simultaneously with these developments is the ever-present influence of in-house systems. Newer, on-line ones, like that devised by municipal data processing staff for the East Brunswick Public Library at a cost of $28,000, probably will be entering the marketplace in the near future. In addition to cost savings, such systems allow the library to tailor design a system for its unique needs. To rival those capabilities, commercial vendors are making software design less proprietary, and a number of vendors now sell software separately.

III

Criteria for System Acquisition

Serious attention to automating circulation accelerated in the early 1970s with the advent of the first packaged systems. While few libraries purchased systems in those early years, several formed committees to monitor developments in the field. For example, in this period the city manager of Greensboro, N.C., formed a group to investigate automation. Almost six years later the Greensboro Public Library decided to automate.

In some cases the wait was for economic reasons. Only special grants or Library Services Construction Act (LSCA) funding made implementation of plans possible. As Richard DeGennaro points out, "In the end the purchase and implementation of such a system may be the single most expensive purchase a library will make."[1] Technological advances, spurring the growth both of internally developed and packaged systems, coupled with decreasing costs, however, have renewed interest in acquisition of such systems. While new products and new vendors with untested product performance pose difficulties, sufficient experience exists to offer at least broad outlines of how librarians arrive at acquisitions decisions.

THE DECISION PROCESS

Surveying the Literature

The first step is to gauge the state of the art by reading the available literature. Such was the drive behind the early automation committees. At present, there are a number of available reports. For example, the American Library Association's *Library Technology Reports* for May 1975, September 1975 and May 1977 cover the then available systems. There is Knowledge Industry Publications' *Advanced Technology/Libraries* newsletter and the Professional Librarian series of monographs. The first edition of this study appeared in that series in 1977.

---

[1] *American Libraries*, April 1978, p. 212.

A report on the experiences of 38 of the 50 public libraries using turnkey, automated circulation systems contracted by the Fairfax County, Va., Public Library and published in June 1978 by the Mitre Corp., found that 47% reported significant operational Problems, but 70% could still say that their system provided the expected benefits. Over three quarters also said they would purchase the same system again.[2]

The Tacoma Public Library has made available the report done for the library in 1977 by Blackwell North America. That report, which sparked some controversy, is a detailed analysis of proposals of the four vendors most responsive to Tacoma's proposal. On the basis of hardware configuration, terminal cost, upgrade implications, central processors, supplies and functional specifications, the consultants decided that while Systems Control offered the most technically sophisticated system, DataPhase was as sophisticated as was 3M's, but at significantly lower cost. At that time, CLSI's programming language was proprietary, and it could not be upgraded to accommodate more than 15 terminals economically. Systems Control was too expensive. DataPhase had two benefits: it was the low bid, and the availability of OCR promised cost savings for supplies, at least $250 a year for 25,000 labels.

In addition, there are several recent journal articles, particularly in *American Libraries,* April 1978. A literature survey does not afford an adequate basis for acquisition in itself, however, for all printed sources are somewhat out of date. What the survey will do is alert potential customers to the general capabilities of systems and the experiences of users.

Requests for Proposals

After obtaining a general notion of what systems can and cannot do, the library staff must analyze its own needs and determine what particular requests it would make of an automated system. Such discussions and planning are part of preparation for writing specifications for bid. The Tacoma Public Library, working in conjunction with the Washington Library Network, developed a list of general specifications. Then the public library differentiated its needs from the network's. The result was a preliminary specification. In other words, Tacoma specified what it wanted, but was open to alternative vendor suggestions. Those tentative specifications afford a good outline of what should be included.

For example, included in the Tacoma *Request for Proposals for a Computerized Library Circulation Control System* are the following sections:

> 1. Acceptable procedures for bids: how forms are to be filled out; to whom questions should be addressed and what factors will determine bid award; a list of vendor's founders, names of company officers; number and type of professional employees; vendor's organization; bank references; annual report; name of investment banker; balance sheets

---

[2] *Automated Circulation Systems in Public Libraries* (McLean, Va.: Mitre Corp., June 1978). Expanded December 1978.

for last two years; Dun & Bradstreet report; opinions concerning last two years' financial statements from a CPA.

2. The library system's operations and history: size; circulation statistics; interlibrary loan relationships.

3. General instructions to bidders: vendors may bid on software only; price is not the sole criterion; a list of users should be supplied, including the quantity of disk storage each requires in relationship to size of collection; vendors should supply a list of supplies needed, including recommended stock level; vendors should detail any site preparations on system standards (turnkey);

4. Functions required — system should: permit charging on initial patron visit; accept varying loan periods; signal when bar codes have not been read; provide a borrower list at certain intervals; have a claims return key; permit circulation of uncataloged materials; interface with WLN data base with full MARC II content.

5. Technical requirements: storage capacity; number of terminals.

6. System configuration: where hardware should be housed, etc.

The Tacoma request also included a notarized non-collusion affidavit, a performance bond and an acceptance test. The latter specified that after the system became operational, it must run for 60 days with less than 2% downtime. The Tacoma proposal also defined the date by which the equipment was to be operational.

Library staff may write the functional specifications, detailing what jobs the system should do and the preferred way of doing them, but some technical assistance is usually required to write the technical specifications. The San Jose Public Library had the help of a city technical agent; the Tacoma Public Library had the assistance of two consultants; the Northland Public Library hired a consultant. At least half of the 20 librarians interviewed for this study employed consultants during some part of the acquisitions procedure. Some libraries are fortunate enough to have municipal data processing personnel or highly qualified technical services personnel already available to them. Others must look outside. The cost is well worth it, for as DeGennaro advises, it is essential to obtain "the advice of experienced consultants the way businesses and governments do when they are faced with similar complex technical, financial, and managerial decisions."[3]

In addition to offering suggestions for technical specifications, consultants play another large role. For instance, the Tacoma Public Library employed a consultant from Blackwell North America, a library wholesaler and cataloging service, to assess bids in

---

[3] *American Libraries*, p. 221.

light of the library's specifications. It was probably because of outside assistance that Tacoma was able to make its purchase decision one month after bid opening. The Northland Public Library hired a consultant for other reasons. While the consultant reviewed vendors' software plans for the library, he also offered both maintenance and, if necessary, ongoing program development and support. In short, good consultants become the library's safeguards, redressing the present disadvantage of librarians in the technical marketplace. Otherwise, DeGennaro characterizes the transaction as "an uneven contest between hard-selling vendors and naive, inexperienced librarian-customers. Not surprisingly, the vendors are ahead."

While specifications are being written, the library should give consideration to the conversion process. If specific vendor assistance is required, that should be included in the specifications. If conversion is going to be handled by a service bureau, bids should be received before or simultaneously with vendors' bids so that a full financial analysis of costs may be tabulated. Writing specifications usually takes about three to four months; the actual decision process varies from one month to two years, with most decisions taking place in about six months.[4]

On-site Visits

After bids are received, the library might choose to make site visits, investigating systems in which they are most interested. Most librarians who have already purchased automated circulation systems highly recommend on-site visits. Important and valuable as they are, however, some caution should be exercised. First, as DeGennaro suggests, "It is particularly dangerous to blindly copy the decision of another library by reasoning that if a particular system was good enough for Library X, then it should be good enough for your library."[5]

Second, the drawbacks itemized by a user may or may not be accurate for any number of reasons. At times, staff misunderstand the nature of certain problems and options available to them. Therefore, the complaints of any user must be taken back to the vendor before an accurate assessment of a system's weaknesses can be made. Third, it should be remembered that libraries that purchased their system several years ago made their decision based on the technology present then; often that technology has changed. For example, when the Dallas Community College District was investigating automated systems, it eliminated C L Systems because at that time it did not offer OCR labels; today C L Systems makes these available.

The site visit may also be used prior to writing specifications. When used in preliminary fashion, it supplements and sometimes updates printed reports relied on for background information.

---

[4] For more on designing requests for proposals, see Audrey Grosch, *Minicomputer in Libraries, 1979-1980* (White Plains, NY: Knowledge Industry Publications, Inc., 1978). Chapter V.

[5] *American Libraries*, p. 221.

ORGANIZATIONAL FACTORS

Furthermore, certain questions such as organizational constraints are rarely addressed. Frequently, automation affects the library's organizational structure. In one large university library, automation meant upgrading the positions of desk attendants operating terminals. Sixty percent of the 38 libraries answering Fairfax County Public Library's questionnaire indicated a reduction in circulation personnel after automation.[6] However, such reductions are but part of the total picture. While one of those libraries reduced a circulation position, it added one in cataloging; another found it necessary to create a totally new position, that of Computer Console Operator.[7] Other libraries, those whose circulation staffs rose after automation, have found it necessary to create new positions. For example, when the Harvey (Ill.) Public Library added book ordering to its CLSI system, two additional part-time clerks were hired. Staff increases are likely when the circulation system is used for more than the traditional circulation functions, which is often the case when such systems permit the library to offer new services. Because the circulation functions have become increasingly complex at Harvey, some consideration is being given to the creation of a new position: Assistant Head of Circulation. Organizational changes depend upon how tasks were performed previously, so the changes effected by automation will vary from library to library. However, they should play as large a role as system capability in the library's decision process.

The decision process itself involves a series of dialogues, beginning with staff from all library departments. Sometimes special on-going review committees to investigate automation developments are formed prior to actual automation. The city manager of Greensboro formed such a committee six years prior to the library's automation of circulation procedures. At other times committees are formed solely to select an automated system and are disbanded after a purchase is made. Whether or not committees are actually formed, extensive staff discussion is essential to assess current systems' capabilities, and more importantly, to clarify what the library wants its system to do. For example, if the data base constructed for the automated circulation system is to be used to prepare bibliographies for patrons, then a system permitting subject access or call number access is desirable. If on-line cataloging is a future possibility, a system with full title file capability is essential. A review of the current literature will define systems' capability broadly; vendors' literature will supply more specific information.

THE FINAL DECISION

The final decision rarely depends on price alone. Important as cost is, system capability and options for future enhancements are vital considerations. Most often, then, costs are adjusted by purchasers to reflect what the system offers. For example,

---

[6] *Automated Library Circulation Systems in Public Libraries*, p. 6.

[7] Ibid, p. 13.

when comparing the various terminals proposed by bidders, the Tacoma consultant also weighed the strengths and weaknesses of each. Likewise, the storage capability of the central processors was compared before prices. Only then do prices become meaningful.

Generally, the current market offers different options with each system. For instance, Systems Control, Inc. (SCICON) and ICC/Plessey are not generally considered cost effective for small libraries requiring few terminals. Gaylord, CL Systems, Data-Phase and ICC/Plessey offer the most packaged systems of hardware and software, but despite certain options, their flexibility is still determined largely by the predetermined parameters set by the vendors. Decicom and Plessey allow a library to begin with an off-line system and gradually convert to an on-line system. Only C L Systems, DataPhase and Universal Library Systems (ULISYS) permit subject access to the data base. Only Gaylord has a true lease option, while other vendors offer a lease/purchase plan. Whether these or other options are advantages or disadvantages depends on the buyer's needs.

SUMMARY

A review of currently available systems often entails dialogue with consultants. Usually data processing personnel will assist in the writing of technical proposals as well as in the analysis of vendors' bids. Blackwell North America, consultants for the Tacoma Public Library, asked vendors to specify whether hardware could be bought directly from the manufacturer by the library, thereby saving the library any middleman costs. Blackwell also analyzed the vendors' bids. Included in any proposals should be some consideration for conversion. Some vendors have not always supplied the best counsel for conversion procedures. Hence, the library must decide what role the vendor should play in conversion. Furthermore, if the data base may be used for future on-line cataloging, some shelflist preparation may be necessary.

After the decision is narrowed to a few vendors, a site visit is helpful. Discussions with other librarians actually using a system prepares the staff to conduct more meaningful vendor interviews. Some caution must be exercised, however, since technology often eclipses problems encountered by early system users. When the search is earnest, the decision process takes anywhere from one month to two years, usually closer to six months. Ordinarily, specifications or proposals for bid take between three and four months.

IV

The Market Today: Available Systems

This chapter describes currently available automated circulation systems, those in operation and those for which bids have been awarded. For each system there is, first, a brief introduction identifying the manufacturer and summarizing major features. There follows a description of the hardware, software, functions, reports generated, conversion assistance, maintenance and service offered by the manufacturer and data security provisions. The cost is also given. Arrangement is alphabetical.

Following the descriptions of major systems is a brief rundown of systems currently available but not yet installed or awarded bids and systems soon to be available.

No attempt is being made to evaluate systems; however, users' comments are covered in Chapter V.

CHECKPOINT/PLESSEY

CHECKPOINT SYSTEMS, INC.   PLESSEY ELECTRONICS LTD.
                                  DATA SYSTEMS

Plessey is a large British-based electronic equipment manufacturing company with marketing or manufacturing facilities in France, the Netherlands, Germany, Sweden, Italy, Spain, Africa, Belgium, Australia, New Zealand, Asia, South America, the U.S. and Canada. Specializing in communications and data-handling systems, the Plessey modular circulation control systems have over 450 users abroad.

Early systems were identified by three levels: O, I and II, which Plessey refers to as modules. They are marketed by Checkpoint Systems, Inc., formerly a subsidiary of Logistics Industries Corporation. Independently owned since 1977, Checkpoint specializes in electronic theft detection systems and automated circulation control systems. None of the circulation systems it markets for Plessey is fully on-line.

Plessey's on-line system, Module IV, not as yet installed in any U.S. library, is marketed by International Computing Co.

Since the systems were introduced in the United States in 1974 there have been four installations: Villanova University (Villanova, Pa., level O); Milwaukee (Wis.) County Federated Library System (level IB); University of Texas, Permian Basin (Odessa, Texas, level IIB); and the U.S. Air Force Academy (Colorado Springs, Colo., level O).

Hardware

Levels O, I and II are characterized by batch processing by central computer. What differentiates them from one another is data-base inquiry capability. For example, the entry level system (O) provides none, while level I provides access to reservation data only and level II to book status. Typically, information is relayed via a hardcopy printer; however, Plessey indicates that all systems can be equipped with visual display units, although no U.S. customers use them.

There are further distinctions among levels. For instance, level I is subdivided further. IA offers from 2,000 to 7,000 records of storage of delinquent borrowers or reserve books; IB offers a disk trapping capacity of 150,000. Level II is also subdivided. IIA holds 300,000 items and IIB holds 250,000 bookstock items on each disk. Four disk units may be used per controller. However, IIB includes a link file for reserves which reduces disk capacity but permits title/copy, accession number or ISBN inquiry.

System configurations are as follows:

Level O can handle 10 input lines from local terminals or remote branches multiplexed out to 30 terminals. This system requires a central control unit and a data capture unit. All level I and II systems can handle up to 64 input lines from local terminals or multiplexed to 192 terminals from remote branches. Both require a central control unit, a data capture unit, a choice of terminal models and an optional bar-code label printer.

The central controller, including the magnetic tape transport and disk store (when applicable), is housed in standard cabinets, usually 6 feet high, 21 inches wide and 30 inches deep. Also contained in cabinets are connectors and power supplies for local terminals and remote branch lines. In level O, trapping store, mentioned earlier, is an optional feature of the control unit.

In level O the data capture unit records all circulation transactions in machine-readable form on magnetic tape reels. Transactions read at terminals reach the data capture unit via the central controller. In levels I and II, operations are controlled by a minicomputer; transactions are relayed by the controller to the tape drive. Data are then ready for central computer batch processing, producing printouts of items checked out and overdue notices. Also available is a portable data capture unit used for remote locations, such as a bookmobile. A battery-operated cassette data tape recorder, the unit records up to 5,000 transactions. The portable includes a keyboard and an attached light pen. Date due stampers are an option for all light pens. Useful as a backup, the portable can include check-digit verification, to assure proper data input. Input is relayed over telephone lines or the cassette may be taken to the central computer.

Two other terminals are available. Model 1130 is for use only when bar codes are available on items and identification cards. It is a light pen terminal dedicated to charge and discharge tasks and may be mounted flush with the circulation desk. Operation is simple, with a number of operational safety features included. To activate a terminal, a library card is placed in the card holder. Patron ID number is read by stroking the light pen over the bar-coded label; should the bar code on the item be read first, the error light will flash. The patron number is read first, then the item label. If the trapping option has been selected for the system, a light will flash on the terminal when either a delinquent patron or a reserve item is detected. All told, there are three lights — ready, error and trap — along with a reset button on the terminal.

The terminal model 1330 has all the features of the 1130 plus a 16 character keyboard and a display panel for verifying input data. It permits all functions (charge/discharge reserve, renew and erase) via light pen or keyboard (if bar codes are not available). Both models allow for date due stampers to be attached to light pens.

SCANNING THE BAR CODE with a light pen with the Checkpoint/Plessey flush mounted 1130 terminal. *(Courtesy Checkpoint/Plessey)*

Depending on the system configuration, a central teletype, local inquiry teletype, reservation printer and bar-code label printer may be needed. All are separate free-standing devices. On the model 2137 Label Printer labels can be keyed in individually or output directly by computer via a suitable interface. The printer computes and prints a check digit for each keyed number. If desired, labels are also available from Checkpoint's Service Bureau.

Hardware for level O and terminals for levels I and II are manufactured by Plessey and serviced by local repair offices run by or contracted by Checkpoint. Central computer is arranged by the library and usually processing is done through a service bureau or through other available computer sources.

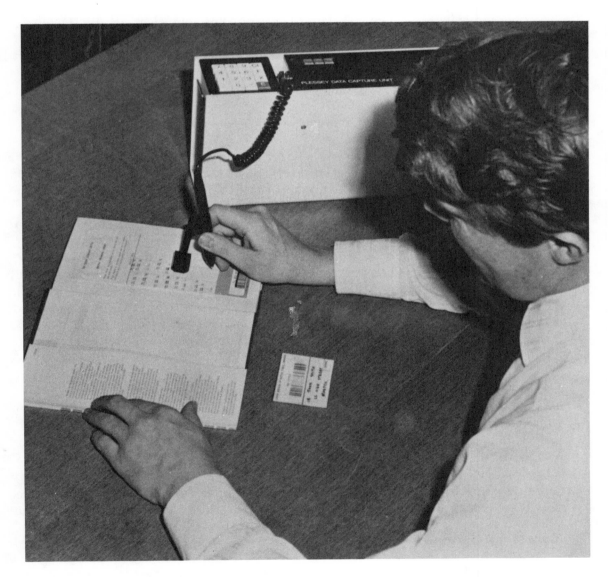

USING THE CHECKPOINT/PLESSEY portable terminal to record a checkout. *(Courtesy Checkpoint/Plessey)*

Software

Checkpoint/Plessey software takes care of all component interfacing from the reading of bar-code labels to the transmission of data via the controller to the data capture unit which is chosen to be compatible with the central computer. In level O, however, constructing borrower and inventory files, maintaining files, processing transactions and printing output is the library's responsibility. All software needed by the minicomputer for processing and file maintenance on levels I and II is provided. End inputs and complete files are the library's responsibility.

Functions

Checkpoint/Plessey's levels O, I and II perform the following:

- identify delinquent borrowers (optional on level O, standard on levels I and II)
- permit renewals and telephone renewals
- place and cancel reserves (optional on level O, standard on levels I and II)
- check items in and out
- permit limited data base inquiry

Trap storage for items on reserve and for delinquent borrowers is optional. In the first module traps must be keyed in manually either after a printed list of delinquents is received or after overdues are visually determined at the check-in desk. Furthermore, while only limited reservation data inquiry may be made on level I, more detailed reservation data is available on level II. Level II permits borrower and item file interrogation, but the extent to which that is possible and the access points available are individually determined. For instance, level II users access item status files through accession number only and have very limited access to borrower files. The latter results from limited storage capacity. Plessey indicates, however, that access to bookstock files is possible through ISBN, title/copy or accession number. Borrower file inquiry is also possible, but only on delinquent patrons. The largest operating public library system in the U.S. is the Milwaukee County Federated Library System, which handles over five million annual circulation transactions.

Level II is on-line as far as transaction recording is concerned; however, access to data is limited. Furthermore, typical features of current on-line systems like fine calculation are absent. For instance, the library staff person can determine whether or not a book is out, seconds after it has been charged out, but data is mostly numerical; that is, a patron's identification number will be printed, not his or her name. There is a substantial gulf between such limited file access and the more sophisticated systems currently available. Furthermore, the on-line capability is not the usual route by which the library lists its circulating items. For that, batch processing is the normal procedure.

Reports and Conversion

Since the Plessey system does not generate a specified number or type of statistical reports, conversion and reports are largely the domain of the library. The programmers responsible for central computer operations, in conjunction with library staff, determine the quality and quantity of statistical data generated. Likewise, conversion techniques and schedules are determined by the library. If required, conversion assistance, including programs for converting machine-readable records to Plessey format, is available with the level IV.

Maintenance and Service

Checkpoint, with main offices at Barrington, N.J., and a major service office in Milwaukee, Wis., provides service for all Checkpoint/Plessey systems. In most instances, Checkpoint arranges for third-party contracts with local firms. But if greater expertise is required, Checkpoint personnel will service equipment. Regardless of third-party contracts, annual service fees are paid directly to Checkpoint.

Data Security

Data security quality depends on system and module. Terminals for all systems have a number of data security features. On most terminals an error light indicates that labels have not been properly read. All terminals, including the portable data capture unit, have check-digit verification, again assuring accurate data input. Also, the level IB system records transactions in two places. It creates a transaction tape and transfers the tape to disk. The disk, therefore, holds a copy of the day's transaction tape along with the previously created master transaction tape.

Cost

The base price for a module O system, including light pen and composite terminals, control and data capture unit is approximately $42,000. Base price for level I is $70,000. The label printer costs approximately $10,000., the portable unit approximately $3,000.

Long-term leasing arrangements are possible.

CLASSIC

CINCINNATI ELECTRONICS

Cincinnati Electronics is a manufacturer that does much of its work under government contract, building communications, command and control, radar and space systems. It is a direct descendant of the Crosely Corp., which manufactured refrigerators, radios, televisions and automobiles.

Its entry into the library circulation field is through CLASSIC – the Circulation Library Automated System for Information Control. This is built around the JRL-1000 terminal developed by the staff of the Joseph Regenstein Library of the University of Chicago. Cincinnati Electronics markets the terminal, having acquired exclusive world rights to its manufacture in December 1975. While terminals alone are still being sold to such customers as the University of Chicago, North Carolina State University and the Texas Medical Center, CE has been marketing its minicomputer-based automated circulation system since January 1978. A year later, the one installation in operation was at the Kentucky Center for Energy Research in Lexington. Additionally, CE has won the Henrico County (Va.) Library System bid for a seven branch system.

CLASSIC is an on-line system based on a minicomputer and utilizing a light pen to scan bar-coded labels affixed to books and library identification cards (OCR-A labels are optional). One medium-sized mini-processor can support 64 terminals, while a total of 256 terminals can be accommodated on the largest computer. Among CLASSIC's operational circulation programs are book and materials reservation and copyright violation. The copyright violation program alerts staff that the library has already made the stipulated number of photocopies allowed by law. The person responsible for library photocopying enters the name and year of the journal for which a request has been received and receives clearance if the library has not already exceeded copyright restrictions.

Under development are programs for acquisitions, serials check-in, interlibrary loan and subject search — on-line catalog. Also in the developmental stage is a microcomputer-based circulation system designed for small libraries. CLASSIC is intended to eventually serve as the basis for a total library automation program.

Hardware

CLASSIC operates on a Sperry Univac V-77 minicomputer. Light pens and terminals are either manufactured by Cincinnati Electronics or are standard, off-the-shelf items. The type of printer supplied depends on the library's needs. In the past Centronic models have been used. By 1979 CLASSIC changed to Printronix printers employing the American Library Association character set.

CE offers many different terminals. The JRL-1000, with light pen and printer, produces receipts for returned materials, prints date due slips, provides a list of fines and a list of currently charged items (if desired) and permits limited inquiries like patron status and obligations. Checkouts are recorded by stroking the light pen horizontally across the bar-coded labels on the books and the patrons' ID card. Returns are transacted by again scanning the book's bar-coded label. If no printed notices are needed upon removal or return of items, the library can use a CS-1100 terminal, which eliminates the printer.

A CRT terminal is needed if the system must handle placing a reserve, renewing a book by telephone, paying a fine (in full or in part), inputing new data or making inquiries of the data base. A variety of terminals are available. If the library so desires, both light pens and printers can be part of the CRT unit. Portable units serve several functions. Being battery operated, they provide backup in case of power failure. They are ideal for small, geographically distant collections like those in bookmobiles. Transactions are recorded onto cassette and added to the data base at a later time.

Overall, hardware configurations are flexible and depend on the library's needs. For instance, JRL-1000 terminals alone can be linked to support systems which the library may already have available. If the library purchases the entire package, the mix of terminals is determined by the library.

Software

The available software package consists of the operating system, which includes FORTRAN IV, Assembler and numerous utilities; TOTAL (the data-base management system); and the applications software package, CLASSIC. CLASSIC is written in FORTRAN IV, a commonly used higher-level programming language. That means two things to the library. If necessary or desired, the library could develop additional software to access the CLASSIC data base; since this does not change the CLASSIC software the warranty is maintained. Second, the library may develop its own programs to run on the system for non-circulation functions.

As with several of the newer automated library circulation system vendors, CE will sell the software alone to a library which already has a computer. CLASSIC can operate on any computer — mini or mainframe — on which TOTAL and FORTRAN operate.

TOTAL is one of several data-base management systems; it is the most frequently used data-base system in the United States. It permits programs written in different programming languages to make inquiries of the same data base. In fact, CLASSIC can operate under TOTAL while application programs accessing an entirely different data base are operating on the same machine. TOTAL permits flexibility and expansion.

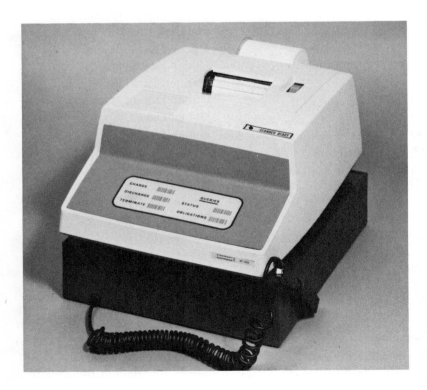

THE JRL-1000 Light pen with a printer. *(Courtesy Cincinnati Electronics)*

THE CINCINNATI ELECTRONICS microcomputer with printer and keyboard in a single unit. *(Courtesy Cincinnati Electronics)*

The CLASSIC concept involves integration of all library computer functions. The following list shows the status of the various CLASSIC packages:

Circulation	Operational
Copyright/ILL Fair Use Control	Operational
Cataloging	Under Development
Acquisitions	Under Development
Serials Control	Planned
Interlibrary Loan	Under Development
Inter and Intra-Library Communication	Under Development
Data Base Reference Interface	Planned
On-Line Catalog	Under Development
Subject Search	Under Development
Books for Blind and Physically Handicapped	Planned
Film and Materials Booking	Final Stage of Development
Networking	Operational
Terminal Contractor	Operational
Security Control	Operational (Checkpoint)
Administrative Processing	Planned
Time-Sharing	Operational
Payroll	Operational
OCLC Data Base to CLASSIC Data Base Conversion	Operational
OCLC-Off-Line Interface	Operational

There are two approaches to OCLC interface. In one, a software package converts OCLC archival tapes to the CLASSIC data base automatically. In the other, a CS-400 Data Terminal, which records data on magnetic tapes, may be connected directly to the printer port on the OCLC terminal so catalog information may be captured and then transferred to the CLASSIC computer.

Functions

CLASSIC performs the following automatically:

- identifies delinquent borrowers
- checks expiration date of patron's card
- alerts patrons to reserves on hold for them
- assures that patrons are eligible to borrow the items they wish to check out (restricted borrowing privileges)
- searches items being checked out to determine whether they are on reserve for someone, whether they have been charged to someone else or whether they were previously reported missing or lost
- calculates correct charge period based on patron, item and terminal
- handles check outs
- produces date due slips
- accepts renewals, including telephone renewals
- handles returns
- places reserves
- calculates fines
- permits partial payment or full payment of fines
- searches patron and material status files; searches patron obligation files
- produces material return receipts, if desired
- produces reserve, overdue, recall and unpaid and overdue notices
- operates a reserve book system, permitting materials to circulate hourly and overnight
- generates statistical reports

Although 2½ years went into its development, CLASSIC is a newly developed automated library circulation system, one particularly responsive to innovations which librarians request. For instance, a reserve book system is part of its circulation package. Because CLASSIC calculates due dates on the basis of time and because the computer's parameters may be set accordingly, books can circulate for any length of time, from 15 minutes to one year, and materials normally circulating for only one or two-hour periods during the day will automatically become overnight books after a specified time, perhaps 5 p.m. The system also permits the reserver to determine when an item will be needed. In other words, the patron can stipulate that a particular item is needed on September 5. CLASSIC will assure that if the item is not circulating, it will never be given a due date later than the time for which it is reserved. If the item is circulating, a recall must be placed. Advance posting of reserve requests allows class reserves forwarded to the library by professors to be entered into the system immediately.

The date after which an item is no longer needed may also be specified. If the item is not available before that date, the reserve is automatically cancelled. If a reserve is cancelled, the system generates a note to that effect for the patron. Generally, reserves are placed either on a title or on a particular copy, and they enter the computer in the same order as placed. The library determines when an excessive number of reserve requests have been made. Should excessive requests be placed, the staff operator is alerted by a printed notice. Furthermore, as in the Gaylord system, reserves may be placed both on a local and on a system-wide basis. A system-wide reserve insures that any copy of an item crossing a circulation desk as a discharge anywhere in the system will trigger a reserve.

An additional concern of librarians is that the patron's right to privacy be maintained; in an on-line system access to patron files is potentially at anyone's fingertips. In the CLASSIC system the library determines a list of authorized personnel and provides it to the computer; only those persons will be granted access to either the patron status or obligation files. The former lists the patron's status (delinquent, items on reserve and items currently charged out). The obligation file lists returned overdues along with unpaid bills and fines.

As an additional safeguard, the CLASSIC system distinguishes between data accessible to patrons and to staff by dedicating terminals to public use and by allowing the library to determine what data should be available at those dedicated terminals. The following kinds of information may or may not be selected depending on library policy:

- whether the item is non-circulating
- if the book is in circulation
- the date the item is due back
- who has the item
- number of copies
- circulation history
- whether the item is lost or missing
- reserves placed on the item — the number and a list of persons in the reserve queue in order

A further advantage CLASSIC offers is that the call number, author, title, a combination of author and title and a patron's name can be substituted when the bar-coded numbers are unknown, as in the case of a renewal when the patron does not physically have the item. A final unique feature of the system is the variety of printed notices which are available. Each confirms a transaction and thus eliminates the arguments frequently heard around circulation desks when patrons claim they have returned materials while the librarian can find no record of the transaction other than the check-out.

A drawback to the CLASSIC system at present is that subject search is still being developed; and when it is available, it will not be offered as part of the basic circulation package.

Reports

The library may choose the type, the format and the frequency of the reports it wants. Examples of statistics available on a daily basis are charges by terminal, charges by terminal by hour, withdrawn materials and reserved materials. A purchase alarm, indicating an excessive number of reserves for an item, signals when that predetermined excessive amount has been reached. Typically available on a monthly basis would be circulation statistics by type of material, patron type, patron class and item classification number. In addition to regularly scheduled reports, data may be manually called by the library. Any regularly scheduled or special report may be called manually. Potentially available are:

- number of charges by charge type
- number of notices by notice type
- current charges and current financial notices of selected patrons
- all unreturned recalls over a specified number of days old
- all books ready for final notice
- all books lost/missing

Conversion

Conversion requires the library to change patron and holdings files to machine-readable form and to affix bar-coded labels both to materials and to patrons' library identification cards. While CE has no facilities to do actual conversion, a certain amount of advisory assistance is available. After consultation with library staff, options can be recommended for in-house manual conversion, hiring an outside firm or loading an already available machine-readable data base into the machine.

Maintenance and Service

Hardware is maintained by Sperry Univac, which has over 8,000 field service engineers throughout the country. CE will route service calls, but direct contact saves time. Cincinnati Electronics includes a warranty on the software at no additional cost even if the library writes its own application programs. However, if the library modifies the applications programs provided by CE, the warranty is adjusted accordingly, in relation to the modification.

Libraries with their own data-processing staff have the option of servicing the software themselves.

Data Security

Check digits on the bar-coded labels affixed to materials and to patron identification cards assure that incorrect numbers will not be read into the data base. The battery-operated cassette portable charge/discharge units, described in the hardware section, may be used as backups. Another backup unit, the data logger CS-400, can be attached to each terminal as a hookup between the terminal and the computer. Should either telephone lines or the computer be down, the CS-400 will capture data which will be automatically relayed to the computer when the system is again operable. When the system is running, it is constantly backed up on magnetic tape, which means that data can be read back into the system if lost because of malfunction.

An additional security measure for larger configurations is the use of dual processors. If a great number of terminals must be supported, two Sperry Univac V-77/400s or 600s can be used in tandem. Neither is enslaved to the other. Therefore, should one be down, the other will assume the functions of the other. Until the other computer is repaired, response time will be somewhat slower than normal.

Cost

Since hardware configurations vary from institution to institution, pricing is difficult to specify. However, a minimum system, consisting of a minicomputer, console, disk drives, magnetic tape, one or two terminals and a printer, would be in the area of $100,000. Individual JRL-1000 terminals are priced at $3,200.

Circulation software by itself sells for $30,000 − $50,000.

LIBS 100 (CLSI)

C L SYSTEMS, INC.

Organized in 1967 as Computer Library Services and reorganized in 1976, C L Systems, Inc. is now employee-owned and currently develops, assembles and maintains the various modules which are a part of its LIBS 100 System. That system comprises acquisition, vendor and fund accounting, materials booking, reserve book room, public access catalog and circulation control modules. While all are part of the same system, each is a separate package. The acquisitions package predates circulation by about a year, having been first marketed in 1971.

Like Gaylord Bros., libraries are CLSI's sole market. Unlike Gaylord Bros., however, the LIBS 100 is CLSI's sole product. In 1977, *Library Technology Reports* indicated that 100 libraries were using LIBS 100. By late 1978 over 250 public, academic and special libraries in Canada and the United States were reportedly using the system. In 1978 alone, 60 new libraries joined the CLSI system, increasing revenues 70% from the previous year.

Marketed in 1972, CLSI's was the first and is now the oldest automated library circulation control system. It is an on-line, minicomputer-based system which requires that a machine-readable data base of patrons and library material be created and barcoded labels be affixed to library materials and patron identification cards (OCR is now an option).

Although fully documented, the system continues to grow, change and develop. For example, in 1977 *Library Technology Reports* noted the following about CLSI's circulation module:

- the system could handle a maximum of 16 terminals

- the programming language, FLIRT, was proprietary, making local modification impossible

- the mode of data-base entry was restricted to zebra number (the number on the bar-coded labels) or to search codes for patron and title

None of those statements was still accurate in 1979. Emplying multiprocessor structure, the circulation module is capable of accommodating several hundred terminals. Present programming structure allows modifications to LIBS 100 programs to be written in BASIC, COBOL and FORTRAN. Lastly, libraries may choose any number of access fields to data bases. For example, access is possible through author, title, subject and call number.* Reportedly, some libraries access patron files through social security number; others access government material through Superintendent of Documents classification number.

A few years ago the LIBS 100 circulation module was differentiated from other automated circulation systems on the basis of its standardized hardware. According to *Library Technology Reports* (May 1977), "With the exception of the first few installations sold by CLSI, all customers have the same computer equipment." That standardization, which facilitates repair, is still pretty much in effect. However, CLSI is also willing to create "specialized products when standard equipment does not meet library needs."

Along with modifications, enhancements frequently update the system, such as:

- development of the laser scanner terminal which eliminates need for a hand-held wand

- development of a portable terminal that relies not on cassettes but on a microprocessor

- addition of a display printer to generate notes simultaneous with transaction

- development of disk-to-tape transfer, permitting production of book and film catalogs

- development of a browsing control which operates by touch

- interface with other data bases such as Brodart's Instant Response Ordering System (IROS)

The laser scanner is not new. In 1975 it was included in Innovated Systems' self-charging, off-line circulation system, developed for the University of Texas at Dallas. However, its use in the recent on-line systems, which rely largely on light pens, is unusual. In addition to eliminating hand-held wands, the laser scanner reduces label wear and reads those in poor condition. According to CLSI, "It reads each label 100 times a second, registering the first good read and insuring a successful read in a minimum amount of time."

---

*Author and title searches may be done by acronym or with a more recent enhancement, by full author or title.

CLSI's portable terminal, for use in remote locations or during power failures as a backup, can store more than 6,000 transactions. The unit is hand held and has no moving parts. Not a cassette device, it is 100% solid state and microprocessor driven.

The printer now available with the CLSI circulation module may be attached to any LIBS 100 terminal. Its functions vary according to the terminal to which it's attached. Fine receipts, routing memoranda, date due slips, bibliographies and shelf-search lists may be generated; any information on the display screen is potential hard copy.

The disk-to-tape capability allows the library to place additional copies of holdings wherever convenient. Film or book catalogs reduce terminal purchase (for example, for dormitories or academic departments). They are ideal for bookmobile use, and when circulated to other libraries, they not only assist cataloging in those libraries, but reduce the interlibrary loan work loads in both.

Introduced during the February 1978 American Library Association Conference, "browsing" terminals for patron use may be placed throughout the library and community and used in lieu of the card catalog. To determine whether the library has a particular item, the patron touches the name of the author, title, subject or other access shown on the screen's faceplate. After the initial search strategy is defined, an alphabetical breakdown is displayed. For instance, if an author search is conducted, the terminal dis-

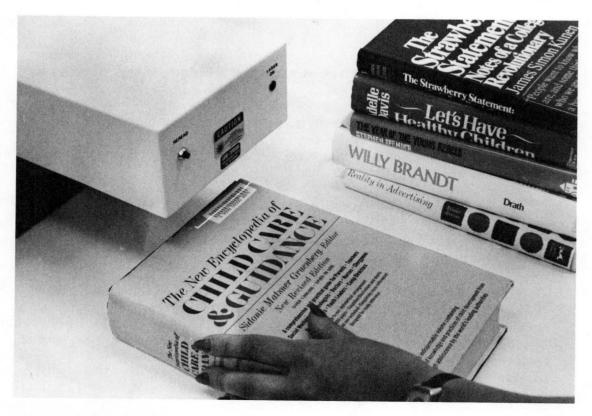

A LIBS 100 laser scanner reads the bar code label. *(Courtesy CL Systems, Inc.)*

THE LIBS 100 browsing terminal allows patrons to search a library's holdings with an interactive process activated by touching the correct response on the screen. *(Courtesy CL Systems, Inc.)*

plays alphabetical ranges, and the browser chooses the appropriate range, A-C perhaps. After the breakdown is made sufficiently narrow, full bibliographic information, status, and location are displayed. As of April 1979 the browsing terminal was not yet functioning in the field. One potential benefit it will provide is minimizing time for patron instruction on terminal use.

The Brodart IROS interface is CLSI's first available library network service. Ordering and searching may be done at the LIBS 100 keyboard/display terminal. Additionally, data stored in the IROS file may be captured and stored in the LIBS 100 file for subsequent use.

Hardware

Minicomputers are purchased from Digital Equipment Corporation. Since all equipment is tested by CLSI, it assumes total responsibility for maintenance. In its early installations, systems employed one of DEC's smaller PDP/11 miniprocessors, either the 11/04 or the 11/05. The DEC PDP/11 series is still the heart of the circulation module, but CLSI now offers over 20 models of the LIBS 100 based on the PDP/11 line of central processors. Storage capacities of the various models range from 20 million to 1.2 billion characters.

Many libraries' circulation modules are based around the PDP 11/04 which provides 56,000 characters of semi-conductor memory, but the 11/34, which provides 128,000 characters, supports a larger number of terminals, up to 64 on-line. Should additional storage and terminals be needed, libraries may expand. The Tucson Public Library, the Salt Lake County Library and the Bear Ridge, Ill., Suburban Library System, for example, have upgraded both processor and storage capabilities.

Although 15 different terminals are available, they fall into one of four categories: light pen stations, keyboard/display units, composite and portable terminals. CLSI's light pen station is dedicated to charge and discharge functions. The keyboard/display unit handles all transactions requiring manual keying, like telephone renewals and data-base inquiry and modification. The keyboard/display units come in 12-inch and 15-inch display tube sizes and they may be combined with either a light pen, OCR wand or laser scanner to form a composite terminal, i.e., one with a scanning device as well as a keyboard/display. Portable units are available for backup and remote location use.

The light pen or OCR wand, like other components, is a standard data-processing item modified by CLSI. Since its introduction to the library market, CLSI has modified the light pen eight times; in one instance the plastic tip of the pen was changed to steel to increase durability.

The optional printer to attach to any display or composite station is an SCI model which prints 2200 characters per second.

Software

The LIBS 100 circulation module is programmed in DEC MACRO assembly language, a standard, high-level language. In the early stages of the module's development, subroutines, controlled by a proprietary language, handled each circulation task. In 1978, however, the RSX-11M operating system was introduced to assure the performance of each task. A standard, real-time operating system, RSX-11M allows the division and allocation of tasks as well as the support of multi-programming capability. Modifications to LIBS 100 programs can be written in FORTRAN, COBOL or BASIC.

DECNET, a communications protocol which allows tasks and files to be divided among system elements, controls inter-machine communication in large networking situations.

Available software offers the library numerous options. For instance, the library decides what terminology will be used in prompts and messages, whether fines should be charged on an hourly or daily basis, what content, format and scheduling are best for reports and which of the 100 loan rules and 100 delinquency criteria should be used. The library also decides what information is included in the data bases; full MARC records may be chosen for the bibliographic data base.* In addition, software permits

---

*These files may be used later for other library applications like the on-line catalog.

communication between terminals connected to the same system, other networks and with separate LIBS 100 systems. Terminals tied to the same systems may be used to relay messages from one branch to another.

For the cost of a terminal and data link, a library not fully on-line to a LIBS 100 may search LIBS 100 data bases. Two Illinois library systems, the six autonomous libraries in the North Suburban Library System (Wheeling) and 11 members of the Suburban Library System (Burr Ridge), have reduced search time and eliminated manual files associated with interlibrary loan requests by networking through the LIBS 100 circulation module.

Functions

The LIBS 100 circulation system can perform the following tasks:

- identifies delinquent borrowers
- identifies borrowers with expired identification cards
- identifies non-circulating materials
- identifies improperly checked in materials
- permits renewals and telephone renewals
- produces receipts and notes simultaneous with transactions
- identifies books on reserve
- places and cancels reserves
- permits patron and item file modification
- relays messages via terminals
- permits data-base inquiries
- determines due date and permits modification
- calculates fines and prints overdue, fine and bill notices
- permits payment of fines in part or in full
- records and compiles statistics for daily use on terminal or for later printed use
- permits patron and item information to be purged automatically
- permits recalls and prints patron recall notices

A sample title inquiry is explained in Figure IV-1.

Reports

All data available in the bibliographic, item and patron data bases may be used to construct reports, with their content, format and scheduling determined by the library. Circulation statistics are arranged by two statistical categories for both patron and item. For example, a public library might prefer items to be arranged by classification number and patrons to be arranged by age, as in Figure IV-2.

On the other hand, as in Figure IV-3, one breakdown preferred by an academic library might be arranging items by branch or division and patrons by status.

Figure IV-1. The Inquiry Process for a Search for Titles by a Given Author

The Title Inquiry Report allows the library to search for all titles on file for a specified author. The circulation clerk enters the author's last name and the LIBS 100 lists all titles on file with the specified author identifier.

KEY:

1 In response to "PROCESS?" question, circulation clerk specifies "inquiry" process.
2 Circulation clerk specifies the "titl" to the "Function?" question.
3 Circulation clerk enters the author's last name. Computer prints out all titles by specified author, including:
4 Full author/title identifier and
5 Title's call number.

OUTPUT:

```
    PROCESS?                          1  inquiry
    Function?                         2  titl
    INQUIRY                           3  lockwood
    Title?
 4  LOCBSRH990
 5  TL448.B8L6
    Lockwood, Tim
    Bultaco:  Service Repair Handbook

    LOCKSRH990
    TL448.K38L62
    Lockwood, Tim
    Kawasaki:  Service Repair Handbook

    LOCMSRH990
    TL448.M18L6
    Lockwood, Tim
    Montesa:  Service Repair Handbook

    LOCSSRH990
    TL448.S8L62
    Lockwood, Tim
    Susuki:  Service Repair Handbook

    Format and details of this and other LIBS 100 displays are determined by the library.
```

Figure IV-2. Report Arranged by Classification Number and Patron Age

PATRON STATISTICAL CATEGORY 1
(Based on Patron Age)

ITEM STATISTICAL CATEGORY 1
(Based on Dewey Classification)

		0-10	11-20	20-40	40-60	60 +	Total
1	0-99						
2.	100-199						
3.	200-299						
4.	300-399						
5.	400-499						
6.	500-599						
7.	600-699						
8.	700-799						
9.	800-899						
10.	900-999						
	Total						

Figure IV-3. Report Arranged by Branch and Patron Status

PATRON STATISTICAL CATEGORY 1
(Based on Patron Status)

ITEM STATISTICAL CATEGORY 1
(Based on Library Branch)

		Professors	Grad Students	Freshmen	Sophomores	Juniors	Seniors	Staff	Total
1.	Main Library								
2.	Reserve Room								
3.	Medical Library								
4.	Law Library								
5.	Art History Library								
6.	Science Library								
7.	Engineering Library								
8.	Music Library								
	Total								

Typical reports generated by LIBS 100 users are:

- circulation count by subject within each branch, including a total count for each subject

- a list of all books circulating more than 50 times, in sequence of descending circulation, grouped by classification number and listed within each branch

- list of books not circulating in shelf order, grouped by classification number and listed within each branch

- list of patrons owing more than a given limit in fines, in order of amount owed within each branch

Conversion

CLSI representatives work with the library staff to develop the conversion strategy most compatible with the library's resources and policies. One of five methods is usually chosen: on-the-fly, magnetic tape, punched card conversion, keypunching or borrowing an existing magnetic tape.

USING THE KEYPUNCH METHOD for converting holdings to computer stored records.
(Courtesy CL Systems, Inc.)

Conversion-on-the-fly is the method used by most LIBS 100 users. As materials circulate, bar-code or OCR labels are attached to the item and book card and to the patron card (if patron data has not been entered previously). Only those numbers need be scanned at checkout time. Later, at the library's convenience, but before the item is due, full bibliographic information is entered. The benefit of this technique is that it allows the library to go on-line quickly: The North Haven (Conn.) Memorial Library became operational immediately after installation.

A few libraries, those anticipating automation, already have holdings and sometimes even borrower records on magnetic tape. Those libraries, like New York University and the University of Wisconsin at Oshkosh, simply had data reformatted to LIBS 100 system requirements through use of the LIBS 100 Magnetic Tape Facility. Using that method, the University of Wisconsin went on-line in the second month after installation.

Two libraries formerly using the IBM System 7, American University and the University of Pennsylvania, loaded previously keypunched cards into the LIBS 100 data base automatically by means of the LIBS 100 Circulation/Conversion Station. Developed by the University of British Columbia Library and Epic Data, the terminal reads bar-coded and punched-card input. Punched book cards and patron IDs are inserted in the station and automatically converted to a format compatible with the CLSI system.

If no prior conversion of records to machine-readable form has taken place, the library may send a microfilmed copy of its shelflist to CLSI for keypunching. CLSI will develop a magnetic tape from the microfilm, creating a bibliographic data base and, possibly, item records as well.

Finally, CLSI and library staff can develop a profile of the library's holdings and search for a library likely to have a comparable collection. By using the Baldwin (N.Y.) Public Library's data base, the Montclair (N.J.) Free Public Library created 80% of its title records without manual keying. CLSI created the Montclair file at its headquarters. Title records were copied off the Baldwin storage disk, but Baldwin item identifiers (bar code label numbers) associated with those titles were erased. At Montclair's check-out, specific item data was recorded by means of the bar-coded labels which were affixed at that time.

Maintenance and Service

CLSI is the sole vendor of an automated library circulation control system which maintains both its hardware and software. The group responsible for software and operational service, the System Group, is reportedly on call 107 hours every week. According to CLSI, the Group solves 90% of all system problems over the telephone. However, when a serious hardware problem occurs, the Group dispatches a CLSI hardware technician. Field representatives carry replacement parts with them: CLSI's philosophy is replace rather than repair.

For an annual fee of $12,000, CLSI will provide service for a configuration of an

11/04 central processor, two 30 megabyte disk drives, four terminals, two composites, one keyboard display and one stand-alone light pen, a fast printer and magnetic tape unit.

Field offices are located nationally in Boston, New York, New Haven, Baltimore, Chicago, Detroit, Houston, Los Angeles and San Francisco.

Data Security

To assure that patron privacy is not violated, restrictions may be placed on certain terminals so that only certain processes may be performed at them. For example, browsing terminals may be used only to make inquiries of the bibliographic data base.

In addition to providing solid state, microprocessor-driven portable terminals for backup, CLSI has two primary backup and recovery programs.

Setcopy: This program records the entire data base on disk. Because the last four days of data are copied to disk, there are four generations of information available for backup at all times. The staff person sitting at the console and operating the program is prompted through the entire process; SETCOPY specifies which disk packs to load and verifies the generation of backup being used.

Recover: This program re-creates the data base by copying from the latest backup version and begins an automatic update of the files. Like SETCOPY, the operator is prompted through the entire process.

Cost

CLSI estimates that the five-year lease/purchase cost for a small library which shares the circulation module in a network would be $625 a month. A large research library holding and circulating over a million items a year would pay $4,500 under the same program. For outright purchase the respective costs would be $38,000 and $280,000.

DATAPHASE
DATAPHASE SYSTEMS INC.

DataPhase was founded in 1975 to develop and sell customized approaches to inventory control, order entry and distributed data collection problems. At present, its exclusive concern is library application. By the end of 1978, 10 libraries had installed or ordered the Automated Library Information System. This system has been chosen by the State of North Carolina for its statewide automated library system.

The product of a study of academic and public library circulation needs, the Automated Library Information System is an on-line minicomputer-based system utilizing machine-readable patron and item inventory files. Having pioneered in the application

THE DATA GENERAL keyboard, light pen scanner and CRT output screen used as part of the Data-Phase system. *(Courtesy Data-Phase Systems Inc.)*

of OCR (optical character recognition) techniques, the DataPhase system requires affixing OCR labels to patron ID cards and library materials for quick data input.

Among the projects still being developed are:

- an acquisitions system to handle all processes from ordering to claiming materials

- materials booking to handle reservations for materials like films and projectors

- a micro-based circulation system to provide smaller libraries with an inexpensive system, including options like MARC compatibility

Hardware

Data General Corporation manufactures the minicomputers, peripheral devices, microprocessors and terminals. In order to offer libraries hardware maintenance policies under original service contract with Data General, Dataphase does not alter the hardware for the library system.

DataPhase library installations rely on the Nova 3/D, the Eclipse S/130 or the Eclipse S/230 lines of Data General equipment. The system selected depends on the size of the library's data base and the number of terminals required, as well as other factors. The Nova 3/D has a memory capacity of 256K bytes; the Eclipse S/130 provides for memory expansion up to 256K bytes and the Eclipse S/230 provides memory expansion up to 512K bytes.

The terminal used most frequently is the Dasher Display 6053, which includes a detached keyboard, swivel and tilt display adjustment, an audible tone to alert terminal operators to special conditions, 11 separate function keys and a hard-copy printer option for production of borrower date due slips or receipts. A serial matrix printer is used to generate "hold availability" and "hold cancellation" and overdue notices as well as the reports the system provides.

Control Data disk drives have been used with large data bases. Other components available with the system include OCR wands, printers and portable cassette terminals for backup inventory and bookmobiles.

Software

DataPhase uses the language and operating system of MIIS (Meditech Interpretive Information System), an industry standard subset of MUMPS, the ANSI-approved language. MIIS permits program development and modification with relative ease. In fact, each system comes with an on-line MIIS teaching manual which instructs operators how to program. For libraries, that means special programs, like payroll and some reports, may be developed on the computer yet be independent of the circulation system.

Because data file organization is highly non-sequential and file structure records are of variable length, DataPhase claims to handle large data bases without impairing response time: under two seconds for 95% of transactions.

DataPhase normally provides the software as part of the total turnkey system, but will sell the software package separately.

THE COMPLETE ECLIPSE S/100 hardware supplied by Data General for Dataphase Systems Inc.
(Courtesy Data General)

Functions

The DataPhase Automated Library Information System performs the following automatically:

- identifies at the checkout delinquent borrowers and those with expired identification cards
- identifies at checkin materials reported as lost, missing, claimed returned, already charged, etc.
- identifies borrowers the library wishes to contact for SDI or other purposes
- permits on-site renewals and telephone renewals
- produces some notices simultaneously with transactions
- places and cancels reserves
- permits patron and item file modification
- relays messages via terminals
- permits data-base inquiries
- determines due date and permits modification
- calculates fines
- generates overdue notices
- permits payment of fines in part or in full
- records and compiles statistics for daily use on terminals or for later printed use
- permits transferral of materials from one library to another on a semi-permanent basis
- checks books in and out

Each circulation task is performed by depressing function keys. In the charge and renewal function, loan period can be adjusted from one hour to any number of days.

Of particular use is the hold function, which permits reserves to be placed on title, edition or copy. Furthermore, patrons may specify hold expiration dates (dates after which they no longer need materials) and branch pickup locations (branches other than the one at which they are registered).

When reserved items are returned to the library, the system will automatically produce a hold availability notice for the first patron in the hold queue as well as display identifying patron data on the screen for the operator. Should the last copy of a reserved item be lost, the system will also automatically issue a hold cancellation notice.

The number of access points to patron and bibliographic files make the inquiry function unique. Patron files may be interrogated by ID (OCR) number and by patron name. Bibliographic files may be accessed by:

- name (main entry personal, corporate or conference names as well as added entry names)
- title
- subject
- LC card number

LIBRARY
LOS ANGELES COUNTY MUSEUM OF NATURAL HISTORY

- ISBN/ISSN
- local call number
- item ID (OCR) number
- separate vendor access numbers

Bibliographic and patron file searches are performed character-by-character. For example, Smith, E. will retrieve matches such as Smith, Eloise as well as Smith, Eugene. The same is true for bibliographic files. Keying in BLACKB will retrieve titles like *Blackberry Bushes* as well as *Blackbirds*. The more precise the entry, the more precise the feedback.

Also noteworthy is the cataloging function, the means by which new items are entered into the system. The system is MARC-oriented and prompts the user by displaying MARC numerical or mnemonic tags. Libraries may store full MARC records or only certain elements of a MARC record.

Reports

Most DataPhase installations are too recent to evaluate user benefits from statistical reports. Typically available are purchase alerts (signaling that a book has been reserved a set number of times indicating its popularity), hold shelf clearance reports (indicating items on hold shelves which are past pickup date) and overdue reports, which list overdue items by amount owed, media and time period. Other management reports are available to profile both a library's collection and user population. Patron reports include registration data (total patrons registered by type, category, status, residence and census tract) and collection usage (patron usage of collection by patron type and media type). Collection usage can be broken down by media type, call number, branch or location within branch. Moreover, the library has the special benefit of being able to program its own reports, after mastering MIIS training.

Conversion

The conversion technique DataPhase used at its pilot site, Tacoma Public Library, was the first of its kind. An abbreviated form with about 1.2 million of the Blackwell North America data base of over 2 million titles was entered into Tacoma's minicomputer. Search keys like LC number, ISBN, author, title and author/title were used to match Tacoma's 250,000 titles to the BNA data-base holdings. When a hit (match) occurred, local item information was also added. By the time the conversion was completed, the BNA data base reflected Tacoma holdings only. At that time BNA upgraded records to full MARC format for inclusion in the Washington Library Network data base. For misses (non-hits), the library keyed data into a newly created data base using standard cataloging techniques and a Tacoma subset of MARC which it calls TACOMARC.

Beginning in March 1979, DataPhase began to market the on-line conversion software in use at Tacoma since February 1978. For libraries whose conversion has been completed by another vendor, DataPhase will reformat the newly created machine-readable records to make them system compatible.

Maintenance and Service

Because DataPhase does not alter hardware in any way, the manufacturer provides for its maintenance. Data General has a nationwide network of more than 125 field offices to handle this service.

To take care of software difficulties, systems have an interface by which programmers at headquarters can dial into the library's system to determine software problems. DataPhase has total responsibility for system operation and maintenance.

Data Security

To assure privacy of patron records, access to patron files is restricted by user passwords. If access is granted, the operator secures personal data (address, etc.), items currently charged, blocks, currently placed holds and items lost or claims returned. To protect records further, the system includes a system security function by which supervisors can add and delete new circulation desk staff as well as control the functions each user is permitted to perform.

To prevent data loss two methods are used: grandfathering and logging. In the first, data is copied from one disk to another (from the current to the master) and stored in a safe place for backup. In the second procedure, transactions recorded on the disk drive are periodically (e.g., every two minutes) transferred to a log on magnetic tape. In case of disk drive failure, log tapes could be transferred to backup disk packs.

An additional backup during power failures or preventive maintenance service is a cassette terminal used at the circulation desk. The cassette with OCR wand attached handles charge, discharge and renewal functions.

Cost

Costs vary depending on the hardware needs of the particular site. For example, the Tacoma Public Library's on-line system required large disk storage; accordingly their system has two 300MB disk drives. With 20 terminals, 600 MB disk storage, 250,000 titles and 30,000 patrons the Tacoma system cost $280,883. A typical minimum configuration would cost approximately $125,000.

DECICOM
DECICOM SYSTEMS, INC.

Decicom installed four circulation systems before quietly abandoning the competition for automated systems early in 1979. Although the system is no longer available, this report still may be useful as a basis for comparing other systems of similar capability.

For over 20 years Decicom's Data Collection Division has been in the business of designing and manufacturing card readers for library and health care systems. The automated circulation control systems which it began marketing in 1974 were an outgrowth of that work. In the mid-1970s, working closely with a group of libraries in the Nassau Library System, Decicom designed a batch processing system which it continued to upgrade over the years.

Although Decicom promoted two separate systems, one totally on-line, the other batch processing with some on-line capabilities, only the latter ever became currently operational. It is being used in four New York libraries: East Meadow, Hewlett-Woodmere, Shelter Rock and North Bellmore Public Libraries. Accordingly, this report emphasizes that system, the Alternative Two/Data Center System.

The system accommodates punched card, bar-coded label or OCR label input. Also, it can support from 30 to 40 terminals, depending on the frequency of terminal use.

Hardware

Decicom manufactured some, but not all of the equipment used in its system configurations. For example, National SemiConductor manufactured the microprocessor.

The basic terminal supports OCR word readers, light pens and a punch-card reader. It was designed and manufactured by Decicom. The OCR unit is also a Decicom product. Other terminals are off-the-shelf. For example, the portable light pen terminal used by Decicom is manufactured by Azurdata.

Software

Decicom software handles all input tasks up to the point that data is recorded on tape. Obtaining software for processing of data, constructing inventory files and determining printed output is the library's responsibility. Decicom offers suggestions, however, and makes printed lists of suggested reports available.

Functions

Decicom's Alternative Two System performs the following:

- identifies delinquent borrowers (optional)
- permits in-person renewals and telephone renewals
- places reserves (optional)
- checks items in and out
- permits data base inquiry (optional)

Basically, the Decicom system is a building block system. In the most simple Alternative Two operations, data is merely captured. Check-ins and check-outs are recorded on tapes which are sent to a data center or central computing center. The large computer produces a printout of all items in circulation. In addition, overdue notices may be generated and certain kinds of statistical reports prepared. If more sophistication is required, a memory system can be included, which permits the library to trap delinquent borrowers and to place reserves on items. To do either, however, manual input of information must be done. For example, using a list of delinquent borrowers supplied by the data center, the library staff decides which borrowers should be trapped and keys in, via the circulation terminal keyboard, those patrons' identification numbers. If a delinquent borrower then attempts to check out additional material, a signal on the terminal lights up. The circulation attendant must then consult a paper file, usually arranged by patron ID number, to determine fines outstanding. Similarly, to input reserve requests, the book number is entered directly into the memory by use of a keyboard.

Reports and Conversion

In the off-line batch mode system, conversion and report procedures are determined by the library. Reports frequently issued are book transaction error listings, book edit and update listings, book inventories and updates, off-line search inquiries and master, update and edit lists of borrowers. Most are issued daily or weekly with the exception of book inventories and borrower master lists which are recommended for quarterly update.

Maintenance and Service

Minicomputers and microprocessers are serviced by their manufacturers. Decicom had provided maintenance of terminals and software for existing installations.

Data Security

In the batch-mode systems, check digits, part of the control numbers, assure that correct data is entered. To assure that certain functions such as file update changes, fine payments and patron data-base inquiries are carried out by authorized personnel only, a special code restricts those operations to supervisors designated by the library.

Cost

Alternative Two, without on-line book status, costs had been priced at approximately $25,000 to $30,000. On-line book status added almost $10,000 to the cost.

THE GAYLORD CIRCULATION CONTROL SYSTEM
GAYLORD BROS., INC.

Gaylord Bros., Inc. is a familiar name in the library world. The company has provided its sole market, libraries, with supplies, equipment, audiovisual materials, systems and furniture since 1896. Gaylord Library Systems, a division of the company, was organized to produce a theft detection and circulation control system. The Gaylord/ Magnavox Book Security System was first marketed in 1976. Its first automated circulation system was installed at the Liverpool (N.Y.) Public Library in December 1975. By the start of 1979 there were nine automated library systems installed at over 110 library locations.

The Gaylord Circulation Control System is an on-line system, relying on light pens to read data into a minicomputer. However, it is different from many of its competitors in several ways. For one, it is based on distributed processing. The minicomputer at the library and the central computer, called the host computer, at Gaylord headquarters in Syracuse divide the various circulation tasks. The library minicomputer handles checkouts, returns, renewals, library reserves and some search functions. The host computer, with which the minicomputer communicates daily to update files, generates overdue notices, recall slips, statistical reports and also continues the search for interlibrary loan requests.

The system's other special features — item control numbers, union catalogs on microfiche, as well as distributed processing — emphasize the system's nucleus: resource sharing. Linking up to the Gaylord system means joining a network. Six digits of each book's bar-coded label are the control number: a unique identifying number, like an LC number, which ties the book into the holdings of all other libraries in the Gaylord system. The control number identifies the same work anywhere. It not only facilitates interlibrary loan searches, but also minimizes the data the minicomputer must store, minimizing response time even with a multiplicity of terminals. The system's minicomputer can support 100 terminals.

In most libraries, even those with some automated system, certain transactions that must be made when a book is not in hand, such as determining whether a book is out or placing a reserve, require locating the control number on the microfiche set of holdings. But in a system such as Gaylord's, the list of the holdings of all libraries tied to the same minicomputer is arranged by title, simplifying the search and making transactions possible even in remote locations, such as in dormitories and bookmobiles.

Modifications and enhancements are being added on a regular basis. Since the last full report on the Gaylord system, the May 1977 issue of *Library Technology Reports,* the following changes have taken place:

- on-line patron and title data has been made accessible from the terminal through a variety of search keys

- systemwide interlibrary loan, in which the host computer searches files of other libraries the same night a book is requested, has been added

- development is in progress for a new system utilizing a data recording terminal instead of a minicomputer

The advantages of the optional on-line patron and title accessibility capabilities are many. First, microfiche is unnecessary. Second, an acronym based on the title may be substituted for the control number when materials are not in hand. Third, on-line patron data means that complete borrower information is available rather than just the borrower's identification (an off-line listing). Access to the file is by patron's last name or by ID number. The Public Library of Columbus and Franklin County in Columbus, Ohio, was the first to use the title data access option. Its system became operational in May 1978.

Gaylord's systemwide interlibrary loan function has always been available; however, only recently has a group of libraries in Onondaga County (Syracuse, N.Y.) begun using the feature. Ordinarily, reserves are in effect only at the location where placed; if no available copy turns up in a few days then the files of other libraries are searched. With a system reserve the files of all libraries are interrogated as soon as the host computer receives notice of a request, speeding up the service for the patron.

The data recording terminal, now under development, transfers information to the host computer nightly. However, the system is not on-line. Although recent trends indicate a greater interest in on-line systems, the off-line system is considerably less expensive: cost will be approximately one-third that of the smallest regular system, or about $10,000. The system is aimed at libraries with circulations of 75,000-200,000. Large libraries tend to find the on-line minicomputer system more affordable and necessary. Conversion from one to the other, however, should be accomplished readily.

Hardware

The typical minicomputer in the configuration is a Digital Equipment Corporation (DEC) PDP 11/34. Each can be provided with core and disk memory to support from

THE COMBINATION KEYBOARD and light pen terminal with CRT display for the Gaylord **Circulation Control System.** *(Courtesy Gaylord Bros., Inc.)*

a few to 100 terminals. Maintenance and service is performed by DEC field service locations. The host facility includes four DEC computers.

The Gaylord terminal incorporates both the light pen and the keyboard/display facility in one unit. The coded labels on books and patron ID cards can be read whether pens are moved from right-to-left or from left-to-right. Light pens record checkouts and returns. The keyboard is used to enter new data, to determine a book's status or availability, to place a reserve, and to request special reports from the host computer. Daily reports, status, and availability data is displayed on the terminal's screen. All terminals are on-line to the minicomputer.

If the title access option has not been selected, the system requires the use of a microfiche reader.

Software

The original software for the Gaylord system was written under contract by Rome Research Inc. a company with background in program development in military and intelligence areas. Gaylord's own staff programmers now manage software.

Programs are written in a high level language as well as in Assembler. System modifications are made by Gaylord programmers, including local options like loan length, fine amount and sequence of systemwide interlibrary loan search.

At the end of the day the library's minicomputer transmits daily transactions, requests for special reports, interlibrary loan requests and new input to the host computer. Based on the updates, the host computer fills interlibrary loan searches, stores information for overdue notices until processing of such notices begins, stores data for weekly, monthly, semiannual, and annual reports and prepares special reports and requests such as the name of a borrower who returned materials in a damaged condition. Except for special requests and daily reports, all available for display on the CRT screens the following morning, reports and notices are printed out through the host computer and mailed to the library or to the patron on scheduled dates.

Functions

The Gaylord system performs the following tasks automatically:

- identifies delinquent borrowers
- displays reason for a borrower's delinquency
- identifies borrowers with expired registrations or otherwise ineligible to borrow certain materials
- identifies a borrower needed for a special reason — perhaps one who left materials in the library
- identifies lost or stolen IDs
- alerts that a loan period is irregular to assure that the proper date due stamp is used

- alters loan period, even for restricted materials
- performs checkouts, renewals, telephone renewals, and transferrals to other library departments such as the bindery
- handles returns
- alerts that unreturned item is overdue, has been returned to the wrong library, is reserved, or is needed by the library
- calculates fines
- permits partial payment of fines and waiving of part or full amount of fine
- signals production of printed recall notices by host computer

For the most part, all functions are automatic. The four files in the minicomputer — item, delinquent borrower, transaction and report — are instantly updated either by means of the light pen or the keyboard. Alerts are displayed on the CRT screen. However, some steps require manual operation. For instance, the CRT will display only the reason for a borrower's delinquency; the full details must be culled from a printed list issued weekly by the host computer. Second, if the system does not have the title access option any function for which a control number is not handy, such as a patron inquiry about a book not on the shelves, necessitates retrieval of a control number from the microfiche list of titles held by the cooperating libraries.

While the distributed processing concept behind the Gaylord system relieves the library of innumerable headaches, it also effects some delays. For example, borrowers are not identified the first time they check-out materials after the expiration of their identification cards. After that initial transaction is relayed to the host computer, however, a stop will be issued and the borrower will be trapped. This compromise was made because stopping only those who use the library, rather than all holders of expired cards, utilizes computer storage more efficiently. A second delay occurs when ordering bar-coded labels. After control numbers are found on the microfiche set and ordered, label delivery takes approximately one week. Should the new item being entered not appear on the microfiche, delivery is within two weeks. Gaylord is developing an alternative which will allow randomly numbered labels to be placed on items, while retaining this common control number link.

Reports

Reports produced by the host computer define holdings, circulation, and utilization of the collection for three designated age levels, by nine different types of material and by up to 500 different subject classes of the library's choice. Patron reports may also define nine patron types and 500 different statistical classes.

Available at any time via the CRT screen are a number of daily reports covering items circulated, returned, and reserved; reserves held too long; cash received from fines; interlibrary loan requests, books sent on interlibrary loan and received; transfer notices and total number of transactions. Weekly reports include:

- new items entered in the data base (the microfiche update of the entire data base appears monthly)

- purchase and exception reports which alert the library that a predetermined ratio of reserves-to-copies has been exceeded and that reserves have not been picked up. Also detailed are the number of books returned to the wrong branch.

- items in status too long — overdues, reserves, interlibrary loans, orders

- items lost, withdrawn or lost

- fines collected and all fine transactions

- a log of activities at each terminal (provided only upon request)

- mailed overdue notices

- supplementary borrowers' records arranged alphabetically by patron's last name (new registration files are issued semiannually)

- new patron data entered in data base

- stopped borrower details arranged by borrower ID number

- reassigned items

- number of interlibrary loan transactions

On a monthly basis a statistical breakdown of the number of items issued by statistical code is provided as well as an updated list of the system's holdings on microfiche and supplementary acquisitions microfiche which list new MARC entries and non-MARC items entered by libraries in the Gaylord system.

Semiannually, the system provides a borrowers' register arranged by patron's name. Six other reports are issued annually: an acquisitions microfiche set lists MARC and non-MARC items entered by libraries in the system; a list of all items which did not circulate; an activity report detailing all transactions at each terminal; a holdings report listing number of titles and volumes held by subject and statistical classes; and a utilization report comparing the ratio of circulation to titles and volumes held. Finally, the consolidated statistical report gives circulation by borrower and item statistical code as well as by broad subject classes. Figure IV-4 is a sample annual circulation report for circulation of adult items in a metropolitan library.

Conversion

As with other computerized systems, the conversion to the Gaylord system involves creating a data base and affixing bar-coded labels to circulating titles. However, Gaylord will convert the library shelflist to machine readable form, integrate that data into the data base, and generate bar-coded labels for all entered items to assist in the conversion process. The cost for those services is 25 cents per title. Total cost to the library must

Figure IV-4. Example of Report Generated by Gaylord Circulation Control System

Gaylord Circulation Control

1980 HOLDINGS ADULT ITEMS
METROPOLITAN PUBLIC LIBRARY

Statistical Class	0-Not Defined	1-Book Hardbd	2-Book Pback	3-Book Lg Type	4-Book Misc	5-Nonbk Records	6-Nonbk Tapes	7-Nonbk Blind	8-Nonbk AV Eqpt	9-Nonbk Misc	Totals
000-Not Defined		1336	165	21				37			1559
001-Mystery		890	95	14				18			1017
002-Science Fiction		1113	126	20				22			1281
003-Western		7785	586	142				165			8678
004-Other English Fiction		860	67								927
005-Spanish Fiction		685	54								739
006-Other Foreign Fiction		4300									4300
007-Spanish Non-Fiction		2900									2900
008-Other Foreign Non-Fict.		3650									3650
009-000-099 Generalities		1206									1206
010-130's Psych. & Occult		3016									3016
011-Other 100-199 Philosophy		1823									1823
012-280-289 Christianity		1265									1265
013-296 Judaism		2785									2785
014-Other 200-299 Religion		25318									25318
015-300-399 Sociology		1218									1218
016-400-499 Language		8655									8655
017-500-599 Pure Science		2355									2355
018-640-649 Home Economics		15643									15643
019-Other 600-699 Technology		675									675
020-770-779 Photography		876									876
021-780-789 Music		3456									3456
022-793-799 Games & Sports		3855									3855
023-Other 700-799 Arts		9855									9855
024-800-899 Literature		2463									2463
025-910-919 Travel		5216									5216
026-920-929 Biography		4876									4876
027-Other 900-999 Geog. & Hist.											
028-Local History		246								56	302
029-Periodicals										612	612
030-Pamph. & Govt. Doc.										186	186
031-Classical						1960	340				2300
032-Spoken Word						296	38				334
033-Children's						498					498
034-Talking Books								111			111
035-Other Recordings					63	2102	420				2585
036-Framed Pictures										60	60
037-Sculpture										22	22
038-Cassette Player									6		6
039-Other AV Equipment									13		13
Totals		118321	1093	197	63	4856	798	353	19	936	126636

include labor for shelflist preparation, taking inventory and labeling. Ordinarily, conversion takes five to six months.

Libraries choosing to convert by themselves follow the same procedure as libraries entering new items and patron input before terminals are installed. Preassigned control numbers must be matched to the items on the shelflist. Then the control number and identifying information are typed on special scannable paper, using an IBM Selectric typewriter. The paper is $20 per 1000 sheets and the scanning charge is 1.5 cents per line. After the sheets are typed, Gaylord enters the library-provided list into the data base at a charge exclusive of labor of about nine cents per item.

Maintenance and Service

All library computer equipment is manufactured by Digital Equipment Corporation. Maintenance for the Gaylord system is provided through DEC's more than 125 field offices. Calls for assistance are placed to Gaylord which in turn notifies the appropriate

CHECKING OUT a patron's books with SCICON. *(Courtesy Systems Control, Inc.)*

DEC office. As part of its maintenance provisions, Gaylord provides one spare terminal for each five operating terminals. Gaylord's own programming staff handles software problems.

Data Security

All digits — item, borrower, and control — include a check digit to assure accurate number entry. If an incorrect number is entered the CRT registers an alert, preventing entry. An audible tone from the terminal assures numbers are valid.

All transactions are relayed to the host computer nightly. Therefore, the central computer, which has a record of each library's activities, acts as a back up. If greater security is required, transactions may be duplicated if two or more disks are part of the minicomputer configuration.

Cost

The Gaylord system may be leased or purchased. A portion of lease payment may be applied to later purchase, so that for a configuration of one minicomputer, one terminal, one microfiche reader with supporting software, including maintenance, fees and insurance, for a library with only one location the leasing cost is $25,000 annually for five years, after which the system is owned. Outright purchase price for the same system would be $36,565. In addition, there are monthly maintenance and fee charges of $825 for the minicomputer and $77 per terminal. A two cent per circulation fee covers the cost of all Gaylord services — reports, statistics, overdue notices, etc.

SCICON
SYSTEMS CONTROL, INC.

SCICON is an on-line, minicomputer based system which requires bar-coded labels be affixed both to library materials and to library patrons' identification cards.

Founded in 1968 Systems Control, Inc. (SCI), with 400 employees, is primarily a software house, designing computer applications for environmental quality, public utility, defense and industrial process control systems. In 1978 it had revenue of almost $20 million.

The library applications staff is relatively small, a group of 10 or 12 responsible for the operations of the automated library circulation control system. SCI entered the library market in 1975 when it won the bid at the San Jose (Calif.) Public Library, a large facility with 15 branches. That system became operational in 1977. Late in 1978 it won the award for the Montgomery County (Md.) Department of Public Libraries contract and in 1979 was given a contract for the Anaheim (Calif.) Public Library. The San Jose Public Library chose SCICON because it was the only system then capable of handling 32 terminals. Although that picture has changed drastically SCICON's market remains the large libraries requiring multiple terminals.

SCICON has since offered the following new features and modifications:

- a data base of San Jose's holdings is now available to facilitate conversion for other libraries

- terminals capacity has well exceeded 32: at present, 256 may be handled

- OCLC members may enter circulation code numbers for new acquisitions during the cataloging process. When OCLC tapes are received all data may be added to the library's data base automatically.

The latter device, invented by San Jose employe Monroe Postman, is available through TPS Electronics (4047 Transport St., Palo Alto, Calif. 94303) for $1675. The unit, comprising a light pen which scans OCR or bar-coded labels and an integrated device with microprocessor, enters circulation code in a unique OCLC field. A specially programmed circulation minicomputer then updates the library's data base.

Hardware

Computer equipment is purchased from Digital Equipment Corporation. Their PDP 11/34 is used if 32 or fewer terminals are required. For a greater number of terminals the DEC PDP 11/70 is used. Digital Equipment Corporation services the hardware.

SCI recommends the use of Monarch light pens. Specifications for other units, terminals and printers are more flexible. For instance, the printers installed at terminals in San Jose proved troublesome, so SCI is looking for other models. Circulation terminal equipment now being bid is a CRT from Lear-Siegler, its ADM/3. Regardless of supplier, however, the SCICON terminal, like the Gaylord terminal, is a composite unit. SCICON refers to its integrated unit of light pen, keyboard and CRT as the Universal Transaction Terminal. A standard part of the system is a printer which provides checkout receipts and other receipts and slips.

The package includes modems to connect remote terminals into the telephone system or local line devices to tie in terminals in the same building. For telephone line connections two options are available. In both instances SCI recommends a four-wire, unconditioned voice grade telephone line to assure maximum system response. There is no cost difference per terminal for the two options, and they may be interchanged.

Software

Programming flexibility is aided by incorporation of the higher level programming language, BASIC. One benefit of using BASIC is that libraries choosing to do so may maintain their own software after the SCI service warranty expires. San Jose, currently under warranty, plans to do so. At that time, SCI will provide complete source code and full program documentation. Thereafter, the library may modify the program as it desires.

SCI also sells the software package alone, for about $40,000. It can also provide programming to interface with other data bases.

Functions

Systems Control, Inc.'s Circulation Control System performs the following tasks automatically:

- identifies delinquent borrowers and those with expired identification cards
- identifies borrowers whose data files are incomplete, who have exceeded the number of material checkouts allowed by the library, or with too many improper checkins
- signals for lost or stolen cards
- identifies a borrower whose fines have been forgiven too many times
- reports on non-circulating materials
- identifies improperly checked in materials
- permits in person renewals and telephone renewals
- produces printed fine and checkout receipts as well as routing slips and other notices
- identifies items on reserve
- permits patron and item file modification
- permits data base inquiries
- places reserves
- records and compiles statistics for daily display on terminals or for later printout
- permits messages to be relayed via terminals
- determines due date, permitting modification
- calculates fines
- permits payment of fines, in part or full
- allows patron and item information to be purged automatically

In operation, light pens record checkouts and checkins. For telephone renewals or other functions requiring keyboard use, operators access the patron file by identification number or by patron key (a code from the patron's name and street address). Item and title files are accessed by identification number, LC number, ISBN number or author/ title key.

SCICON, like ULISYS, provides a HELP command. At any point during a transaction, operators can type HELP on the keyboard and receive a list of various instructions designed to help them complete a transaction. In addition, two other distinct prompt levels are provided: brief and extended. The brief mode, for use by experienced operators, speeds up the system's response time because only abbreviated messages are displayed. Operators less familiar with either the system or an individual function of the system can have more detailed prompts displayed in the extended mode. Shifting from the brief to the extended level may be done at any time.

SCICON offers a number of other features. For instance, to effect quick checkout for newly registered borrowers, only minimal information need be initially entered into the patron file: patron key, name, residence code and ID number. Full data entry may be completed at a later, more convenient time; all borrowers with incomplete records will be trapped when they try to check out additional library materials.

Furthermore, patrons are not fined even if materials are improperly checked in. Instead, a "default checkin" is posted. After a certain number of these, the patron will be trapped when checking out library materials. Staff may then explain proper checkin procedures. The system also keeps track of the number of books a patron has charged out. If that number exceeds the allowed amount, the borrower is trapped. The limit depends on patron category.

In SCICON, renewals may be done on the basis of title or patron. In other words, individual items may be renewed or, with patron renewal, all items charged out to a particular patron are renewed. In the latter case, items will all be due the same day, providing, of course, neither reserves have been placed nor outstanding fines are due although both qualifications may be overridden by the operator. Reserve cancellations are handled similarly.

Certain materials, such as those with duplicate author/title keys, LC numbers, ISBNs and those the library chooses to link together, like repair manuals for Fords, may be tied together in the system. Such linking facilitates reserve requests: after entry and display of all titles and those linked to those titles, the librarian decides whether to place a reserve on either a particular title or a linked list. If the latter is selected, a patron having requested a Ford repair manual receives the first available book. More-over, returned books that are reserved ordinarily go to the next requesting patron. However, if one patron is willing to pick up the item at the branch to which it was returned, that patron is given priority.

In addition to reserve features, patron and item purge programs can be run at the library's discretion. Patrons, book and other materials may be deleted manually at any point. A patron may also be removed from the data base automatically using parameters such as a card unused for specified period, no fines owed, or some minimum amount owed. Values are variable and may be changed at the library's discretion.

Finally, like CLASSIC, CLSI and Innovated Systems, SCICON provides a number of printed receipts to verify transactions. Checkout receipts, cash payments receipts, routing slips and others are available, using printers attached to terminals.

Reports

Various programs in the SCICON system are responsible for generating reports. Basically, reports are of three types: patron notices, statistics, and collection management and development. Overdue, reserve and refund notices are produced intermingled and presorted by zip code. Bills for lost materials are produced in three groups separated by amount owed. Depending on the amount, bills can be mailed, phoned or delivered by messenger.

Patrons granted special loan periods may be sent letters as reminders. Also, patrons, faculty or staff with special borrowing privileges will be notified when reserves are placed on materials in their possession. Letters to staff are produced separately for in-house routing.

Statistical output reports on the number of:

- circulations (extended loan periods are included)
- item checkouts and checkins
- new patron registrations
- renewals
- reserves trapped, placed and cancelled
- fines paid in kind
- delinquency overrides
- overdue notices sent
- bills for lost items
- patron turnaways (trapped patrons who decide not to continue a checkout)
- dollars in fines collected and forgiven

Also available is a circulation report which shows items currently in circulation by branch, including system totals breakdown by call number. Another report summarizes monthly circulation totals for previous 24 months and calculates percentage changes between corresponding months in previous years.

Managerial and development reports are numerous. Printouts are available of special patron checkout, reserve materials not picked up after notification, unreturned reserve materials, overdue ephemeral materials, materials in transit, lost items, patrons owing fines over a given limit, and items and patrons purged categorized by type of delinquency, number and total cost of unpaid lost material bills, call number, author and total fines owed.

Patron lists by class are available to aid in developing the library's collection. Such lists define the universe of borrowers. Moreover, excessive reserves on specific library items or requests for materials not owned by the library can also be spotted through computer reports. Finally, an inactivity program lists all titles of items with low circulation, over a specified period of time.

Conversion

As in other automated circulation systems, a machine-readable patron and holdings data base must be created. To assist in preparation of the latter, SCICON includes the data base of 300,000 titles from the combined holdings of three large public libraries as part of its standard automated circulation control system. According to SCI, with this approach "an encoding rate of about 100 items per hour per terminal can be anticipated." If exact matches are not found, modifications can be made. According to SCI, "This procedure is faster than original entry which is used for those titles . . . not found in either the data base or BALLOTS/OCLC."

As previously mentioned, OCLC members may search that data base for either retrospective or new cataloging entries, simultaneously encoding circulation data. BALLOTS may also be searched, so the standard SCI system contains full software support for use of OCLC or BALLOTS archive tapes. After matches are made and/or modified, bar-coded labels are affixed to items. Unless archive tapes include item information, permitting automatic recording, such information may be added later. That information — ID number, owning agency, price and call number — is added by accessing through LC number, ISBN or author/title key.

Items found in none of the data bases must be keyed in manually.

Maintenance and Service

Digital Equipment Corporation services the hardware it supplies. Depending on configuration, maintenance fees for an 11/34 range between $87 and $147 a month. SCI maintains terminals directly or establishes service contracts with local companies. In addition to Palo Alto headquarters, offices are maintained in Washington, D.C. Software may be maintained under a warranty by SCI or may be maintained by the library.

Data Security

SCICON has a thorough backup system. A log tape of all daily transactions is made as each occurs. Moreover, at the end of each day a tape copy of the disk files is made. If disk file contents are lost, a combination of the duplicate disk file and log tape permits complete reconstruction.

Cost

A minimum configuration with two terminals would cost approximately $150,000. Additional terminals on the basic system are about $5000 each. But a very large system with 80 or 90 terminals and additional memory and speed would be closer to $1 million.

To date, software has not been sold separately. However, it is valued at about $40,000.

While a straight leasing arrangement is not available, there is a standard, five-year lease/purchase option.

ULISYS
UNIVERSAL LIBRARY SYSTEMS, LTD.

Universal Library Systems (ULS) specializes in computer-based systems for libraries. Its only product at present is ULISYS, an automated circulation control system originally developed for the University of Winnipeg. Since ULS' formation in 1976 four ULISYS systems have been installed, two in United States libraries, the latest being at the Northland Public Library in Pittsburgh. Also under development by ULS are two additional systems for acquisitions and film booking.

ULISYS is an on-line system based on a minicomputer and utilizing a light pen to scan bar-coded labels affixed to books and to library identification cards. Depending on the size of the minicomputer, up to 63 terminals may be linked to one processor. Since the Northland installation, ULS has added one new feature: the Digital VT-100 terminal. More important than its variant-sized letter and its blinking to attract the operator's attention to special messages is its ability to store patron number and book number from the bar-coded label or OCR label and/or the keyboard for up to 2700 transactions independent of the computer. In the event the computer becomes inoperative, terminals can remain in use. All new systems include the VT-100.

Hardware

Computer hardware is supplied by Digital Equipment Corporation, which is also responsible for its maintenance. The size of the DEC minicomputer depends on the collection size, circulation and specifications of the library. The existing installations have used the PDP 11/34, the PDP 11/40 and the PDP 11/70.

While processors vary, terminals are all the same. Current systems use the VT-50 and VT-52 terminals. Like the Gaylord terminals, these include a CRT display screen keyboard and light pen in one unit. The newer VT-100, to be used in the future, has the keyboard separated from the CRT. This allows the library to decide what physical arrangement is best. Light pens are made by Monarch.

A basic configuration includes:

- DEC PDP 11/34 CPU with 96K words of core memory
- 2 x 14 megabyte disk drives
- 300 lpm printer
- 800 BPI magnetic tape; (TU10)
- DEC VT-100 terminals with Monarch marking system light pen scanners (number dependent on library requirements)
- Console terminal
- Communications interfaces to hook up CRT terminals

Software

Operating system software, DEC RSTS/E, is supplied and maintained by Digital Equipment Corporation. Applications software is supplied and maintained by Universal. ULS will also sell just its applications software to any library with computer using RSTS/E operating system software.

The applications software for ULISYS is written in BASIC. As has been noted previously, BASIC offers the advantage over other higher level languages permitting relatively easy modification to programs as well as local maintenance. For example, neither report formats nor the amount of book data which is to be on-line is predetermined; the library decides both. At the latest installation in Pittsburgh, the reference staff decided to include the quick or ready reference file in the data base under subject headings, making it easy for patrons to locate desired material.

For libraries with their own programming staff or academic data processing departments, local maintenance may be especially desirable. At the Phoenix Public Library, ULISYS's first U.S. installation, the minicomputer servicing over 32 terminals (there are 10 branch libraries) is centrally housed downtown in a data processing center. Both software and hardware are maintained by that staff.

ULS also indicates that programs are constructed in a modular fashion and commonly used routines are maintained in a subroutine library. This means that a program can be readily modified for a particular library, with only one or two changes being necessary.

Functions

The ULISYS system performs the following functions on-line:

- identifies delinquent borrowers
- identifies patrons who have not picked up reserve materials
- verifies that materials are available for loan
- computes due date (if a due date falls on a day when the library is closed the due date becomes the next date that the library is open)
- permits extension of loan periods
- permits reserves to be placed on materials
- checkouts
- calculates fines
- permits partial payment of fines
- processes renewals and telephone renewals
- transmits messages to other branches via terminals
- maintains and updates every 15 minutes the activity statistics for each branch and each terminal
- processes returns
- permits changes in the patron and book file
- searches in the data base for status and availability of both materials and patron information

Off-line, the system performs the following:

- updating and maintaining of search files (author, title, patron)
- processing of overdue items, preparation of notices
- back-up of master file data onto magnetic tape
- extraction, summary and recording of data for preparation of statistical reports
- preparation of notices to advise patrons of reserved books awaiting their collection

ULISYS is an easy-to-operate system. If the operator is unfamiliar with the required codes, the word HELP can be typed on the keyboard and the codes will be displayed. In all functions, questions directed to the operator via the terminal are in non-technical English.

Holds may be placed in one of two ways. If entered by title, all copies of the item will be put on reserve. When the first copy is flagged, the reserve is removed. To place a reserve or hold on a particular item, the accession number must be entered on the keyboard (the accession number is the unique number represented by the bar code).

Extending the loan period is accomplished by one of two procedures. The first is a simple renewal. The computer responds to the operator's identification of the book and asks the operator to confirm that the renewal should take place. If the extension is requested over the phone, the patron must know his or her identification number and the title or accession number of the book.

One of the benefits of the system is that on-line inquiry of the data base is possible through many access points. Not only is accession number entry possible, but also call number, author, title, subject, and patron's name. Title entry is by actual title, not acronym. Of course, each option requires additional storage capability and that adds to costs. One other bonus is that the switch from checkout to checkin takes less than one second by passing the light pen over a special bar code on the terminal.

A potential drawback to the system is that access to the data base through title, author and subject is delayed until files have been updated off-line. Frequency of updating is up to the library. New data is recorded immediately, but until off-line processing has been completed, access to that new data is through accession number only.

Reports

The number and type of reports the ULISYS system generates is determined by the library. The Arizona Public Library receives the following on a monthly basis:

- registration reports, by type of borrower card (e.g., faculty, student, special)
- patron circulation, by type of borrower card
- circulation by classification number and by zip code for each branch

Conversion

Conversion entails the creation of a data base for the library's holdings and the library's patrons. Both United States installations have preferred to convert in-house; however, ULS is willing to write programs to convert records already in computerized form. Another form of assistance is a matter of instructing staff how to enter data on the terminals.

Maintenance and Service

Digital Equipment Corporation, which supplies the hardware for the ULISYS system, maintains both the equipment and the operating software. Typical service charges for DEC's standard coverage are between $87 and $147 a month for systems designed around an 11/34.

ULS supplies spare Monarch light pens. To service the applications software, ULS is on call 24 hours; oftentimes, problems can be resolved via a telephone consultation. Since ULS is a small company, the training program for library staff is limited and there may be some delays in maintenance repairs.

Data Security

After every reading by light pen of a bar-coded label the terminal produces a beep, assuring the operator that data has been properly recorded. As in other systems, check digits minimize entry of incorrect numbers to the system.

In addition, transactions are logged onto a disk file which is then copied to magnetic tape. The library determines at what intervals the copying on magnetic tape should take place. The data security measures, like so many other functions of the system, are determined by the library managers.

Cost

Since much of the ULISYS is customized, prices vary considerably. Software prices begin at around $18,000 to $20,000. Hardware prices start at $85,000. Some caution should be exercised when gauging a system's price by the cost of previous installations. For instance, in 1977 the Phoenix Public Library paid $350,000 to install a ULISYS system. Hardware prices have decreased since then because of technological advances; the price to install that system today would be a little over $200,000.

ICC/PLESSEY
INTERNATIONAL COMPUTING CO.

International Computing, a systems consulting and product marketing house which designed and implemented New York City's off-track betting system, presently employs 50 people and has offices in Bethesda, Md., and Dayton, Ohio. Revenue in 1977 was $2.1 million, and the company has been growing at the rate of 50% to 75% a year. It markets the British-based Plessey Telecommunications' most current and only fully on-line circulation control system, the Module 4. Previous off-line and partially on-line modules are available from Checkpoint Systems, Inc.

Like the Systems Control System (SCICON), Module 4 is designed for large, multi-branch libraries and is not cost effective for small configurations. Minicomputer based, Module 4 can handle 256 terminals, 98 branches, 2 million items and 1 million registered patrons. A one-second response time is promised up to a loading of about 9000 transactions per hour. In addition to checking materials in and out, the bar-coded label light pen system also renews library materials, traps delinquent borrowers, traps reserve materials, identifies borrowers with expired registration cards, alerts operators to books not on record or already checked out, indicates when borrower limits are reached, calculates fines, permits partial and full fine payments, relays messages via terminals, places and cancels title and item reserves, permits data base updating and data base inquiries. Access points are patron ID number, patron name, title, author, LC or Dewey number, item ID number and ISBN. Like other systems, the Module 4 stores statistical data and generates not only overdue notices and statistical reports but also recall, item available, reserve cancellation and patron status notices.

Hard copy printers produce date due slips, fine payment receipts and routing slips for items on hold. OCR is not an option, and the software is the proprietary CORAL 66, the national standard in Great Britain.

Module 4, while currently available, is not as yet installed in any United States library. Approximate cost for a 10-branch, 20-terminal configuration is $300,000.

INNOVATED SYSTEMS
INNOVATED SYSTEMS INC.

Innovated Systems is a computer systems company specializing in oil field and traffic control. In the early 1970s, when the staff at the University of Texas at Dallas Library (UTD) wrote specifications for an automated circulation system with security features, conventional supply houses told the library staff the project was impossible. Only Innovated Systems responded. The system it designed to meet those specifications became operational in 1975 and remains the only installation for Innovated Systems.

The unique features of the UTD system are the result of the library's primary objective to reduce personnel costs. At present, one or two clerks and student assistants staff the circulation desk, and since the system is a self-charging one, they are often free for other tasks. Director of Libraries, James T. Dodson, estimates that "the library is saving 200 man-hours a week in security staff alone."[1] The 3M Tattle-Tape Book Theft Detection System is part of the system.

Based on the Hewlett-Packard 21MX minicomputer, the UTD system performs the following tasks automatically:

- identifies delinquent borrowers
- prevents books on hold from circulating
- provides for unaided patron check-outs of materials
- signals desensitization of detection strips
- issues a date due slip

The self-charging process is simple. Patrons insert ID cards in a card reader. If the computer determines that the borrower is in good standing, a message on the CRT instructs him or her to place material in a book tray and a laser scanner reads the bar-coded labels, and if no reserves have been placed on the material (other than by the patron checking the item out), the system desensitizes the detection strip placed in the book to eliminate its unauthorized removal. A thermal printer then issues a date due slip to the patron.

---

[1] "Mini Helps Library Users Borrow Books," *Computerworld,* May 24, 1976.

One drawback to the system, but not to UTD users at present, is that it is an absence system, recording items on loan only. That means that it cannot handle inquiries regarding a book's status: whether it is out, lost or overdue. The system is designed to check books out automatically, not to provide an inventory of the library's holdings.

At intervals determined by the library, transactions are transferred to another computer for batch processing. At UTD the interval is every two or three days, using an IBM 370 model. At the end of each day, hold notices are transferred to the main computer which prints and mails them to borrowers. Hardware maintenance is the manufacturer's responsibility; the library maintains its own software. After designing the system, Innovated Systems turned the basic plans over to the library which has its own programmer and data processing supportive staff.

In addition to the UTD system, Innovated Systems planned to release full information about its microprocessor-based circulation control system in 1979. It is designed for medium-size operations, with about 10,000 monthly transactions.

KNOGO
KNOGO CORPORATION

Early in 1978 Knogo announced its agreement with Automated Library Systems, Ltd, a British firm, to jointly produce an on-line combination security and circulation system. Knogo's sole business is the manufacture and leasing of anti-pilferage detection systems. ALS has a number of off-line automated circulation systems installed throughout Europe, Canada and New Zealand. In fall 1978 its first on-line system was installed in a 50-branch library in London.

Knogo plans to wait until ALS's software package is fully developed before marketing their joint product. If all goes as planned, Knogo and ALS will be actively marketing the system by late 1979.

Although comparable to the Innovated Systems' automated circulation system used at the University of Texas at Dallas, the Knogo/ALS system differs in two ways. First, special reader-type labels placed inside the back cover of a book are used instead of relying on bar-coded labels. Labels are scanned after being placed in a book tray, at the same time the theft detection strip is being desensitized. The Knogo unit responsible for those functions, the verifier, is part of the scanning device. Second, unlike the UTD system, the Knogo/ALS system is a totally on-line inventory system.

CIRC
NETWORK SERVICES
UNIVERSITY OF TORONTO LIBRARY AUTOMATION SYSTEMS

CIRC (Collection, Inquiry, Reporting and Communication) is one part of the University of Toronto Library Automation System's (UTLAS) integrated library system. An on-line minicomputer based circulation system, it not only handles checkins, checkouts and renewals, but also places and cancels reserves, calculates fines and records full or partial fine payments. Access points for data base inquiry are patron name, patron ID number, author, title, call number and item identification number. Software is a proprietary package, and user written modifications invalidate the warranty.

The system has several special features. One terminal permits unaided patron checkouts and prints a date due slip. The system handles short-term loans of one hour or less and permits reservation of special materials like films. An on-line search function is printed off-line. It can be used to compile statistics or produce bibliographies (e.g., all items in the collection by a particular author).

Like the Gaylord system, CIRC works on the principle of distributed processing. Thus, certain functions like on-line catalog inquiry and circulation control are handled by local minicomputers. However, functions requiring access to a large data base like searching, cataloging and interlibrary loan rely on a central computer system which can be contacted via a low cost communications link.

Since UTLAS also supplies a catalog support system (comparable to OCLC's) to over 500 individual libraries, it has developed a conversion technique. Libraries submit minimal data from non-machine-readable records using OCR techniques, and UTLAS searches for MARC records in its data base. Record editing is on-line and includes conversion from MARC to CIRC-formatted records.

CIRC will eventually serve a network of 46 libraries across Canada. After successful on-line implementation at the University of Toronto's undergraduate library, the system will be marketed in the United States. In the developmental stage are serials check in, order/acquisitions and cataloging functions.

V

Users' Comments

With the withdrawal of Decicom in early 1979, there were seven on-line automated circulation control system vendors. Although Cincinnati Electronics (CLASSIC) had been awarded the contract for the Henrico County (Richmond, Va.) Library System and the system was being installed at the Kentucky Center for Energy Research in Lexington, it was not operational at that time. Decicom's off-line system was installed in several New York State libraries, but no on-line systems were in operation when it decided to drop out of the business. Similarly, a few Checkpoint/Plessey off-line systems were in use, but no ICC/Plessey on-line systems were. As in earlier surveys, the most thorough user response came from CLSI customers. Since CLSI was the first commercially available packaged system, its users have had greater experience with it than the customers of more recent systems have had with theirs.

Twenty-one libraries using the currently available automated circulation control systems were contacted. Among them were four Gaylord users, one CLASSIC user, five C L Systems users, three DataPhase users, two Decicom users, one Systems Control user, two Universal Library Systems users and three Checkpoint/Plessey users. They were asked the following questions:

1) Why did the library want to automate circulation?
2) How long was automated circulation considered?
3) When the search for a system became serious, how long did it take the library to decide on the system presently used?
4) Why was the present system chosen?
5) How long has it been in use?
6) What are its strengths?
7) What are its weaknesses?
8) What circulation system was used previously?
9) How was conversion handled?
10) What has the staff response been?

11) Has automation affected staffing patterns? Are fewer staff members needed?

12) To what uses are statistical reports put?

13) Is service satisfactory?

14) Does the library have other automated systems?

15) Have there been attempts to interface the automated circulation control system with other automated systems? If so, were there difficulties?

Without exception, users were pleased with their systems and cited their major advantage as superiority over the previously used manual charging system. An additional bonus was savings in staff time, not always realized as staff reduction, but in most cases allowing staff to be reassigned to other pressing tasks. While system strengths were thus generalized because users frequently had minimal knowledge of other automated systems, as a basis for comparison, system weaknesses of their system were more specific. The 21 interviewees assessed those weaknesses as follows:

CHECKPOINT/PLESSEY

Checkpoint/Plessey Levels O, I and II customers cite the following difficulties:

- static interferes with equipment operation, in some cases causing data loss;

- only 80 spaces are allotted for the author/title field, which means that full title data is not always available and that the data base could not be micro-filmed in case the catalog is closed;

- there is an unacceptable amount of downtime.

The vendor response to those criticisms is as follows:

- In England, where Plessey equipment is manufactured, static was not a problem. Since installing systems in foreign countries Plessey has had to deal with the problem. According to John Pearce, director of automated circulation systems at Checkpoint, the condition has been rectified. Equipment has been modified; furthermore, anti-static mats and sprays help to eliminate the problem.

- Since Checkpoint/Plessey does not design host computer software, field lengths are determined by the library and its data processing staff.

Customers close to Checkpoint headquarters rate service as "very good." Others who depend on local service firms for assistance indicate that service representatives are not familiar enough with equipment to provide effective service.

Despite difficulties, no users are considering the purchase of another system or enhancement of the present one: a substantial financial investment in the level of service provided has already been made.

C L SYSTEMS INC. (CLSI)

System weaknesses reported by some CLSI users are as follows:

- limited data field (does not permit full identification of government documents or large multi-volume research sets);

- reserves may be placed on titles only, not on particular copies;

- reports on fines can be organized only by book, not by patron;

- statistical report parameters are limited;

- some information on the title level might be placed more advantageously on the item level (e.g. price and paperback/hardcover);

- development of enhancements is slow.

Vendor response to criticism is as follows:

- an improvement introduced in December 1978 accommodates full MARC format;

- another enhancement will have two hold functions, one for title and another for copy;

- built into the new software is the capability of determining report frequency and parameters in-house;

- if the library is doing an item search it would be more convenient to find necessary information in the item file; however, transferring too much information to item files clutters them, resulting in other difficulties;

- to assure maximum efficiency, C L Systems tests all equipment in-house and all enhancements in pilot libraries.

Service evaluations varied from "very good" to "unsatisfactory." However, all contacted users felt that service quality was impeccable and that there was improvement in the time it took to respond to calls for assistance.

While no libraries had conducted cost-benefit analyses, one user reported the first year was a financial disaster because equipment and staff conversion needs were underestimated. Another library, using C L Systems Acquisitions and Circulation modules, reported some savings: the circulation system cost slightly more than the previous semi-automatic system, but the acquisitions system less.

DATAPHASE

At the time of this report most DataPhase systems were in operation for only a few months. Given this limited experience, service ratings were good and no libraries reported system weaknesses.

With newly operating systems, a review of selection criteria may be more helpful than premature performance evaluations. The Tacoma Public Library based its purchase decision on its consultant's report, the *BNA Consultants Report*. Not all vendors were evaluated in that report, only those submitting bids for the Tacoma Public Library. DataPhase had two strong selling points: software sophistication and reasonable cost. Other purchasers have also chosen DataPhase for software sophistication, one noting that DataPhase's programming language is recognized by the American National Standards Institute. One other acquisitions advantage was that DataPhase made OCR available before other vendors.

Two users reported substantial staff reductions through attrition. One large public library lost five staff members, another eliminated three to four full-time positions, a third felt the system would pay for itself in five years.

DECICOM

Decicom's on-line system was never installed and having abandoned the market it apparently will not be. The current users have Decicom's Alternative Two/Data Center batch processing system. Alternative Two users indicate that when terminals were developed they were troublesome. There was no way to assure that data was being recorded or recorded accurately. Because of inadequate controls, terminals were unreliable. According to users these problems were eliminated after modifications in 1976.

Users rate both system performance and service as "very good." All customers are situated in New York, as is Decicom. Those contacted had planned to stay with the company, upgrading systems with Decicom enhancements, including full on-line capability, but this was prior to Decicom's announcement on dropping out of the competition.

GAYLORD

Gaylord users mentioned minor equipment failures such as light pen breakdowns and some software difficulties causing inaccurate recording of fines. Such software problems characterize early installations. At present service is rated "satisfactory."

No system design weaknesses were reported by those contacted. Most users chose Gaylord for its particular design — one permitting interlibrary loan networking and central computer report and notice production. One library selected Gaylord because it's the only system available on a lease basis. Also, on the plus side, most users report circulation staff decreases. Despite present satisfaction, users suggest that the early conversion technique — microfilming shelflists for keypunching in Taiwan (arranged through AutoGraphics) — produced poor results.

SYSTEMS CONTROL INC. (SCICON)

SCICON's sole operational installation is a large public library with 15 branches, the San Jose Public Library. San Jose cites only two weaknesses: response time is five seconds rather than the one-second response they had been promised, and the printers are poor. Presently the library is obtaining new ones.

Systems Control was one of two vendors able to meet San Jose's specifications, which included printed date due slips, printed routing slips for items routed among branches and system-wide reserve capacity. Service is satisfactory, and San Jose expects to pay for its $465,600 system within three years. One contributing factor to savings is that 17 positions have been eliminated through attrition.

UNIVERSAL LIBRARY SYSTEMS (ULISYS)

ULISYS's two United States customers are extremely satisfied both with system performance and with service. Only one drawback was mentioned: ULISYS has no training program.

The Phoenix Public Library selected the system because it could handle a large number of terminals; they began with 26 and have added six more. The Northland Public Library decided on ULISYS after determining that both hardware and software maintenance could be handled by local firms and consultants if necessary. Other decision criteria were involved as well. ULISYS supplied Northland with a larger minicomputer than competing vendors at no substantial cost increase.

VI

Implications of Automated Circulation

TECHNOLOGY

There are no technical developments on the horizon likely to alter the basic design of current automated circulation control systems. For the next few years microprocessors will remain devoted to the support of off-line systems. And while OCR (optical character recognition) labels will eventually eclipse bar-coded labels because they are less expensive to produce and may be produced in the library, the technology for them is hardly new, having preceded that of bar-coded labels in the mid-1960s.

The real innovation in system design is already available: increased flexibility. For example, C L Systems Release 24 (commonly called Version 2) plans to incorporate a report scanner and a report generator that will allow the library to set the parameters in-house for the kinds of reports it wants. The scanner selects parameters, the generator selects the physical format and frequency with which it is produced. This capability should be available by the end of 1979.

The present locus of system flexibility is the separate sale of software and library maintenance of software. In the past, libraries with access to computers had to design their own automated circulation systems. Also, packaged systems made it impossible for libraries with access to systems analysts and programmers to employ them in system maintenance or modification. Neither is still true. Newer vendors have provision for library software maintenance and enhancement. Even C L Systems, still a strongly packaged system, offers the optional capability of modifying software, although it maintains that few customers demonstrate an interest in the option.

Originally, the Kentucky Center for Energy Research in Lexington planned to design its own system, since hardware was already available to them for other operations. Eventually, however, it purchased system software and terminals from Cincinnati Electronics to operate its circulation system on the existing computer. The Kentucky Center is just one of the libraries benefitting from the increased options design flexibility makes possible.

TECHNOLOGY AND THE SMALL LIBRARY

For the small library, one with an annual circulation of between 50,000 and 200,000, a variety of inexpensive microprocessor-based circulation systems are either available or are about to be introduced. Presently available are Gaylord's Micro I and III. Both are off-line systems in which daily transactions such as charges, discharges and fines paid are transmitted to the host computer at Gaylord on a weekly basis. Transmission is by telephone lines. At the host facility files are updated and reports such as overdue notices, reserve and borrower reports and data and management control reports are generated. In both systems, there is no direct access to data on file. Purchase price is $4,500 for the Micro I and $5,250 for the Micro III. The latter includes a memory that allows entry of patrons wanted for consultation for excessive fines or overdue materials and of titles wanted for reserve. Leasing arrangements are also possible. For example, a library with an annual circulation of 75,000 could lease a Micro I for $725 a month, including monthly maintenance and transaction fees for processing. Comparable monthly charge for a Micro I that was purchased is $575 a month. In both instances, fees would be slightly lower for circulation figures under 75,000.

Three other systems are currently under development. In mid-1979 Innovated Systems planned to release details on its microprocessor-based system designed for libraries with a monthly circulation of 10,000. Cincinnati Electronics is working on an on-line absence microprocessor-based system. Finally, Gaylord plans to release Micro V. That system will permit data base inquiry, will instigate reserve and stop alerts automatically and will be in daily communication with the host computer.

At present, the microprocessor-based systems do not offer the same capabilities as minicomputer-based systems. No microprocessor currently provides total inventory control and complete data base access. However, the new microprocessor-based systems bring the efficiency benefits of automation of circulation economically to the small library, and in a few instances, they may also make it less costly than manual operations.

RESOURCE POOLING

While automated circulation system prices have decreased, a $100,000 investment is still beyond the budget of many libraries. Resource pooling lowers cost substantially. Because it makes such sound economic sense, it is destined to provide a cost-effective way for small libraries to automate. For example, the 13 member libraries of the Suburban Library System (Burr Ridge, Ill.) pay only $750 a month for the first five years and $280 a month thereafter to share four CLSI LIBS 100 systems. Ken Sheedy, Vice President of Universal Library Systems, indicates that it might cost $120,000 for a computer to operate in one library with four service points, but only $400,000 to run several libraries with a total of 40 service points. To maximize savings, libraries should be geographically close, reducing telecommunications expenses. There are on-going maintenance savings as well. For example, there is only one administrative center to store the computer. And there are also service and other benefits. Interlibrary loans as well as cataloging may be facilitated through such resource pooling.

Although system sharing is not feasible for the large library, both small and large libraries are using automated circulation systems for a number of cooperative, networking ventures. As far as established networks go, the Washington Library Network (WLN) partially funded the Tacoma Public Library's acquisition of an automated circulation control system from DataPhase. The $54,652 grant was given so that Tacoma could serve as a pilot site for other member libraries and a prototype circulation subsystem for the network. The network will benefit in yet another way. When Tacoma's conversion is complete, its data base will be added to the data base at WLN, expanding the scope of WLN's present bibliographic subsystem.*

UTLAS, the University of Toronto Library Automation System network, which serves 46 Canadian libraries, has devised its own on-line circulation system. Also to be part of an on-line cataloging system, CIRC (Collection, Inquiry, Reporting, and Communication) was developed as the system's software and will eventually be marketed in the United States. The system is more than just an automated circulation control system. Circulation, acquisition control and eventually serials check-in are handled by local mini-computer systems; network functions like searching, cataloging and interlibrary loan which require contact with the central system are conducted via low-cost communications links.

OCLC, a third established network for shared cataloging, has plans for implementing a circulation system. Although this is a long-standing commitment, plans are still in the developmental stage. Both New York University and San Jose Public Library (CLSI and SCICON users, respectively) have developed ways to enter circulation control numbers simultaneous with the cataloging of new items. And DataPhase is developing a means of taking information from OCLC screens and transferring it to circulation terminals so information can be entered directly into the circulation system data base. As yet, that is the present scope of interface between the OCLC network and automated library circulation system users.

Still in its early operational stage is CLSI's interface with Brodart's IROS program (Instant Response Ordering System). IROS is an on-line order service for in-print U.S. books which is available on a monthly fee basis. A librarian can search the central IROS book order information files on IROS terminals. If an item is in print, the order key on the terminal is depressed and a six-copy 3x5 order form with full bibliographic information is printed automatically, which is then sent to Brodart for fulfillment. The CLSI/Brodart interface signals the direction automation is taking as well as the central, pivotal role circulation plays in that development.

---

* Tacoma loaded an abbreviated form of the Blackwell North America data base into its computer. The data base so formed is sent to BNA for full MARC II upgrading and is then added to WLN's data base.

For example, LIBS 100 terminals can be used to make inquiries of other LIBS 100 data bases to facilitate interlibrary loan. Such reciprocal searching is utilized by the Suburban and North Suburban Library Systems in Illinois, between the University of Nevada (Reno) and the Clark County Library District (Las Vegas), as well as by members of the State University System of Florida. While it has not purchased a packaged interface nor participated in an official network, Pittsburgh's Northland Public Library plans to expand the usefulness of its automated circulation system (ULISYS). In-house, the computer will be used to contact computers at Baker & Taylor, Brodart and BALLOTS. Library director Laura Shelley envisions partial automation of many new manually performed library functions through the circulation system. For that reason, subject access to the data base was included in the system so that reference staff could use the computer to answer some reference questions. On the outside, the library is encouraging the local school district to purchase terminals and acoustical couplers for school libraries to make possible on-line inquiries to Northland. The logical extension of this idea is the installation of terminals in office buildings and in other strategically located public access areas.

Since the days of off-line batch processing of checked-out materials, circulation systems have made considerable progress. The necessary conversion of holdings to machine-readable form is having residual benefits, such as enlarging central bibliographic data bases. Telecommunications links now enable groups of libraries to form their own communications networks easily and to contact other network data bases with relative ease. While still in its infancy, the trend of automated circulation systems is toward the exploitation of data bases for networking possibilities, despite the resistance of a few librarians who prefer simple in-house supervision of charge/discharge and overdue tasks. The reality of the trend is seen in the Systems Control, Inc. interface for networking with similar and dissimilar computers (IBM, CDC, Univac, DEC, etc.) and in the concentrated interest in pooling resources. It is shown in the Greensboro (N.C.) Public Library's DataPhase circulation control system with five other libraries, with central facilities located at the Greensboro facility. And it is manifest in the Kansas City (Mo.) Public Library's decision to make its CLSI data base its shelflist as soon as it receives call number access.

GENERAL COLLECTION CONTROL

Networking efforts are in their infancy, as are other automated circulation control system capabilities. For example, in 1977 a review and evaluation of the then available systems concluded that "even after much talking and writing, there has still been no significant effort directed toward building a truly usable capacity in the area of extracting management information from circulation systems."[1] To a great extent the truth of that statement reflects the library's commitment to circulation as circulation and its desire to maintain traditional organizational structure. In part, however, the statement reflects the infancy of automated circulation itself. Conversion, staff training, system

---

[1] Bill Scholz, "Computer-based Circulation Systems — A Current Review," *Library Technology Reports* 13:234 (May 1977).

implementation and efficient system operation preclude attention to additional system services. In time, that will change. All interviewed librarians were either using or planning to use statistical data generated by the circulation system to define clientele, determine acquisitions, prevent duplicate acquisitions, determine hours of greatest volume at particular terminals, to signal purchase alerts for items in particular demand, to determine library hours and to weed the collection. Thus, statistical data will be taking an increasingly active role in collection development and control rather than just a passive record-keeping one. One other positive collection control benefit, reported by the Mitre Corporation, indicates that 65% of 193 contacted public libraries showed a reduction in loss of library materials after use of an automated circulation system.[2]

---

[2] Simpson, p. 7.

VII

Conclusions

Automated circulation benefits are well known. For one, they eliminate the burdensome task of filing, the heart of a manual system. Before converting to an automated circulation control system, a busy day at the Commack (N.Y.) Public Library resulted in a half day of filing book cards for staff members. Photographic systems were better in one respect. Although libraries no longer knew whether a book was charged out, at least filing was eliminated. However, photographic systems left the library with yet another chore: preparation of overdue notices. Automated systems eliminate both, simultaneously providing better service. Whether the system relies on batch processing or is on-line, overdue notices may be generated automatically and on a much more timely basis than either manual or photographic systems permit.

One large advantage of such streamlining is that circulation staff is free to do other tasks or, more likely, may be reassigned to different departments. Users of automated circulation control systems agree they can now get more work done without hiring additional staff. New York University's experience offers dramatic proof. In the year after installing a circulation control system, circulation reportedly increased 243%, but no additional staff was required to handle the load.

Another advantage automation provides is new services. One of the most attractive new features is catching delinquent borrowers when they try to take out another book. The more sophisticated systems also provide signals at the checkout desk for borrowers whose registrations have expired or whom the library may wish to contact for any other purposes. In manual and photographic systems, after overdues were issued, lists of delinquent borrowers could be compiled, but catching delinquents entailed checking all patrons against the list. The same one-by-one process, checking all returns for tagged cards, was necessary to flag reserve books, a task on-line systems perform automatically.

Automation also increases the circulation department's data collection ability. Most systems can be programmed to alert the library to books which have not circulated for a predetermined length of time, books reserved a given number of times, reserve books not picked up in a specified number of days, the number of transactions per terminal at any given hour and a wide variety of statistical breakdowns for books in circulation. Such reports help the library make discard and purchase selections, determine library hours and staffing patterns.

Such benefits notwithstanding, few libraries have actually automated circulation. Some cite cost and technical expertise, others size. Initial investment, purchase and ongoing maintenance costs for automated circulation control systems are often beyond a library's budget. A typical on-line system costs about $100,000 and that's exclusive of telecommunications, records conversion and maintenance costs. Supplies and system expansion and enhancement are another sizeable expense.

Additionally, systems handle journals in a variety of ways. Usually there are two options. In one a bar-coded label unique to that issue is affixed and the journal discharged. If it is overdue, the library knows only that a particular patron has a journal with a particular bar-coded label outstanding. The title and volume are not known. That procedure satisfies public libraries, but not academic ones. The second option entails input of specific journal data before its discharge. That is handled in a variety of ways. DataPhase is currently working on a system of separate OCR labels for each volume. Systems Control allows a title record of 255 characters in the item file. C L Systems permits copies to be indicated on a title record or separate title records for each volume. The latter is more popular. Gaylord has accomodated journals at least three different ways. Similar situations arise for non-print items. Using MARC format, DataPhase establishes a different loan period for each type of media. C L Systems is developing a distinct number for different types of material. Inability of systems to process materials other than books is another explanation for limited library commitment to automated circulation.

Furthermore, if an automation committee has not been previously established, library staff must begin the time-consuming, arduous task of reviewing available literature and familiarizing itself with the market and puzzling through vendors' promises and performance. A number of key decisions must be made before the library begins writing specifications: mode of access, OCR or bar codes and reserve capacity, to name only a few. Sometimes the help of a consultant is essential, especially in the design of hardware specifications. Both staff time and consultant time represent an added financial investment, one few libraries are willing to make.

For some, the investment is not necessary. If manual systems are operating efficiently and there are no dramatic increases in circulation to impair system efficiency, there is little motivation to automate. Such libraries may devote a portion of staff time to keeping abreast of developments, preparing for future changes.

Despite financial drawbacks, interest in automated circulation systems grows. The reasons for such are numerous. For one, system sharing (using one minicomputer to accommodate several libraries) reduces system costs substantially. Furthermore, hardware prices have decreased over the years. While the conversion process is never trouble free, greater experience with conversion in the last few years offers the library a broader range of choices, some much more sophisticated than those previously available. For example, the Tacoma Public Library's conversion process was heralded as a landmark approach. (See p. 50.)

Increased vendor competition provides another boost to library interest in automating circulation. When the first report on automated circulation control system was released in 1975, five vendors were reviewed. Two years later there were still five vendors, but only two of the previously reviewed systems were still available. That particular market change represented the trend away from off-line to on-line systems, rather than any increased competition. However, today there are seven vendors of on-line systems, and two more companies have announced plans to enter the market. Some additional ones have demonstrated potential interest, and a number of developers of home grown systems are in the process of entering the market, such as the East Brunswick (N.J.) Public Library and Ohio State University, whose LCS system is currently being implemented at the University of Illinois.

Increased competition has made vendors more responsive to library needs and demands. In an attempt to capture as much of the library market as possible, some vendors now:

- allow separate software purchase;

- permit libraries to maintain software, and thereby to add or modify programs as they choose;

- offer OCR as an option;

- design inexpensive microprocessor based off-line systems for small libraries.

Networking continues to spur interest in automating circulation. The cooperative ventures of most networks are facilitated when member libraries have holdings in machine-readable form. That is the first step in automating circulation and it opens doors to shared cataloging, faster interlibrary loan procedures and cooperative materials selection plans.

Lastly, automated circulation is becoming the hub not only for cooperative networking ventures but for total library automation. The ability to contact other data bases like BALLOTS, Lockheed or Baker & Taylor enhances automated circulation's desirability. To date, interfaces with all these systems have not yet been firmly established, nor do automated circulation systems handle all problems, e.g., serials-checkouts. Library automation is not the answer to all library problems. Nevertheless, automated circulation has become one way of solving one of many libraries' major bottlenecks while at the same time preparing the way for broader application of the data base acquired.

APPENDIX

DIRECTORY OF MANUFACTURERS OFFERING AND
LIBRARIES USING AUTOMATED SYSTEMS
(current to January 1, 1979)

1. CHECKPOINT/PLESSEY
Checkpoint Systems, Inc.
110 E. Gloucester Pike
Barrington, N.J. 08007
(609) 546-0100

U.S. Installations

MILWAUKEE COUNTY FEDERATED LIBRARY
   SYSTEM
Milwaukee, Wisconsin
(Milwaukee Central Library
814 Wisconsin Ave.
Milwaukee, Wis. 53233)

U.S. AIR FORCE ACADEMY at COLORADO
Academy Library (DFSLB)
U.S. Air Force Academy, Colo. 80840

UNIVERSITY of TEXAS/PERMIAN BASIN
Odessa, Tex. 79762

VILLANOVA UNIVERSITY
Villanova, Pa. 19085

Canadian Installations

CARLETON UNIVERSITY
Ottawa, Ontario K1S 5B6

YORK UNIVERSITY
Toronto, Ontario M4N 3M6

2. CLASSIC
Cincinnati Electronics
2630 Glendale-Milford Rd.
Cincinnati, Ohio 45241
(513) 563-6000

KENTUCKY CENTER FOR ENERGY RESEARCH
Laboratory Institute for Mining and Minerals Research
P.O. Box 13015
Lexington, Ky. 40583
(606) 252-5535

Contract bid awarded in late 1978 for
HENRICO COUNTY LIBRARY SYSTEM,
Richmond, Va.

3. LIBS 100
C L Systems Inc.
81 Norwood Ave.
Newton, Mass. 02160
(617) 965-6310

ALAMEDA COUNTY LIBRARY
224 W. Winton Ave.
Room 108
Hayward, Calif. 94544
(415) 881-6337
Ms. Barbara Boyd, County Librarian

Includes the following on-line libraries:

Fremont Main Library
Centerville Library
Union City Library
Irvington Library

ALBANY PUBLIC LIBRARY
161 Washington Ave.
Albany, N.Y. 12210
(518) 449-3380
Mr. Edgar Tompkins, Director

ALSIP-MERRIONETTE PARK LIBRARY DISTRICT
11951 S. Crawford Ave.
Alsip, Ill. 60658
(312) 371-5666
Ms. Margaret S. Schmitt, Director

American University
BATTELLE-TOMPKINS MEMORIAL LIBRARY
Massachusetts & Nebraska Aves., NW
Washington, D.C. 20016
(202) 686-2320
Mr. Donald Dennis, Director

ARLINGTON HEIGHTS MEMORIAL LIBRARY
500 N. Dunton Ave.
Arlington Heights, Ill. 60004
(312) 392-0100
Mr. Frank Dempsey, Executive Librarian

AURARIA LIBRARY — See Colorado, University of

ANDERSON, M.D., MEMORIAL LIBRARY,
See Houston, University of

AUSTIN PUBLIC LIBRARY
401 W. Ninth St.
P.O. Box 2287
Austin, Texas 78768
(512) 472-5433
Mr. David Earl Holt, Director

Includes the following on-line libraries:

Manchaca Road Library
Windsor Village Library
North Village Library
Montopolis Library
Old Quarry Library
Mobile Station Library
Terrazas Library
Twin Oaks Library
North Loop Library
Carver Library
Oak Springs Library
Howson Library
Southwood Library

BALDWIN PUBLIC LIBRARY
2385 Grand Ave.
Baldwin, N.Y. 11510

(516) 223-6228
Mr. Walter Haber, Director

BALTIMORE COUNTY PUBLIC LIBRARY
320 York Rd.
Towson, Md. 21204
(301) 296-8500
Mr. Charles Robinson, Director

Includes the following on-line libraries:

Towson Library
Cockeysville Branch
Randlestown Library

BATELLE-TOMPKINS MEMORIAL LIBRARY —
See American University

BLOOMFIELD TOWNSHIP PUBLIC LIBRARY
1099 Lone Pine Rd.
Bloomfield Hills, Mich. 48013
(313) 642-5800
Mr. H.G. Johnston, Director

BOISE PUBLIC LIBRARY
715 Capitol Blvd.
Boise, Idaho 83706
(208) 384-4466
Mr. William F. Hayes, Director

Brigham Young University
HAROLD E. LEE LIBRARY
University Hill
Provo, Utah 84602
(801) 374-1211
Mr. Donald K. Nelson, Director

BROOKLYN COLLEGE LIBRARY
Bedford Ave. @ Ave. H
Brooklyn, N.Y. 11210
(212) 780-5335
Prof. John Herling, Director

Brown University
JOHN D. ROCKEFELLER LIBRARY
Prospect Street
Providence, R.I. 02912
(401) 863-2162
Prof. Stuart C. Sherman, Acting University
    Librarian

California State University, Sacramento
LIBRARY
6000 J Street
Sacramento, Calif. 95819
(916) 454-6466

Mr. Gordon P. Martin, University Librarian

California, University of, Davis
SHIELDS LIBRARY
Davis, Calif. 95616
(916) 752-2110
Mr. Bernard Kreissman, University Librarian

California, University of, Los Angeles
UNIVERSITY RESEARCH LIBRARY
405 Hilgard Avenue
Los Angeles, Calif. 90024
(213) 825-1201
Mr. Russell Shank, University Librarian

Includes the following on-line library:

Biomedical Library

California, University of, Riverside
UNIVERSITY LIBRARY
P.O. Box 5900
Riverside, Calif. 92507
(714) 787-3221
Ms. Eleanor Montague, University Librarian

Includes the following on-line libraries:

Physical Science Library
Bio-Agricultural Library

California, University of, Santa Barbara
UNIVERSITY LIBRARY
Santa Barbara, Calif. 93106
(805) 961-2674
Mr. Allen B. Veaner, University Librarian

CAMBRIDGE PUBLIC LIBRARY
449 Broadway
Cambridge, Mass. 02138
(617) 876-5005
Mr. Joseph G. Sakey, Director

CARLSBAD CITY LIBRARY
1250 Elm Ave.
Carlsbad, Calif. 92008
(714) 729-7933
Mrs. Georgina Cole, Director

CHESHIRE PUBLIC LIBRARY
104 Main St.
Cheshire, Conn. 06410
(203) 272-2245
Ms. Susan Bullock, Director

CLARK COUNTY LIBRARY DISTRICT
1401 E. Flamingo Road
Las Vegas, Nev. 89101
(702) 733-7810
Mr. Charles Hunsberger, Director

Includes the following on-line libraries:

Las Vegas City Library
West Las Vegas Library
James R. Dickinson Library, University of Nevada
    Las Vegas
Learning Resources Center, Clark County
    Community College
Decatur Library
Sunrise Beach Library

Clark County Community College
LEARNING RESOURCES CENTER
3200 E. Cheyenne Ave.
North Las Vegas, Nev. 89030
(702) 643-6060
Mr. Frank Gafford, Director

Colorado, University of
AURARIA LIBRARIES
Lawrence at 11th St.
Denver, Colo, 80204
(303) 629-2805
Dr. Donald E. Riggs, Director of Libraries

Includes the following on-line library:

Denison Memorial Library, Medical Center

COOK MEMORIAL PUBLIC LIBRARY DISTRICT
413 North Milwaukee Ave.
Libertyville, Ill. 60048
(312) 362-2330
Mr. Frederick H. Byergo, Director

COOPER UNION FOR ADVANCEMENT OF
SCIENCE & ART LIBRARY
41 Cooper Square
New York, N.Y. 10003
(212) 254-6300 X 322
Mr. Fred H. Graves, Head Librarian

D.C. PUBLIC LIBRARY — See MARTIN
LUTHER KING MEMORIAL LIBRARY

DECATUR PUBLIC LIBRARY
247 East North St.
Decatur, Ill. 62523
(217) 428-6617
Mr. Robert H. Dumas, Director

DOLTON PUBLIC LIBRARY DISTRICT
14037 Lincoln Ave.
Dolton, Ill. 60419
(312) 849-2385
Ms. Mary H. Zenke, Director

DOWNERS GROVE PUBLIC LIBRARY
1050 Curtiss St.
Downers Grove, Ill. 60515
(312) 960-1200
Mr. Joseph H. Quady, Director

EDMONTON PUBLIC LIBRARY
#7 Sir Winston Churchill Square
Edmonton, Alberta
Canada, T5J 2V4
(403) 423-2331
Mr. Vincent Richards, Director

EISENHOWER, MILTON S. LIBRARY —
See Johns Hopkins University

EISENHOWER PUBLIC LIBRARY DISTRICT
4652 N. Olcott St.
Harwood Heights, Ill. 60656
(312) 867-7828
Ms. Susan Biskup, Director

ELA AREA PUBLIC LIBRARY
13 S. Bussching Rd.
Lake Zurich, Ill. 60047
(312) 438-3433
Ms. Elizabeth Bishoff, Director

ELMHURST PUBLIC LIBRARY
Wilder Park
Elmhurst, Ill. 60126
(312) 279-8696
Mr. Lawrence Knudsen, Director

ELGIN (Ill.) PUBLIC LIBRARY — See GAIL
BORDEN PUBLIC LIBRARY DISTRICT

ELMWOOD PARK PUBLIC LIBRARY
4 Conti Park Way
Elmwood Park, Ill. 60635
(312) 453-7645
Mrs. JoAnn Carbery, Director

ENERGY LIBRARY
Division of Library Services
Department of Energy
Washington, D.C. 20545
(301) 353-4301
Mr. C. Neil Sherman, Director, Division of
Library Services

Includes the following on-line library:

Energy Library, Germantown, Md.

ERIE CITY AND COUNTY LIBRARY
3 South Perry Square
Erie, Pa. 16501
(814) 452-2333
Mr. Kenneth Sivulich, Director

Includes the following on-line libraries:

Edinboro Library
Lawrence Park Library
Millcreek Library
Southeast Library
Harborcreek Library
Liberty Library
Presque Isle Library

EUREKA-HUMBOLDT LIBRARY
636 F St.
Eureka, Calif. 95501
(707) 445-7513
Mrs. Judy Klapproth, County Librarian

Includes the following on-line library:

Arcata Library

EVANSTON PUBLIC LIBRARY
1703 Orrington Ave.
Evanston, Ill. 60201
(312) 475-6700
Mr. Donald Wright, Director

Includes the following on-line libraries:

North Branch Library
South Branch Library
West Branch Library

FAIRBANKS NORTH STAR BOROUGH
LIBRARY AND REGIONAL CENTER
1215 Cowles St.
Fairbanks, Alaska 99701
(907) 452-5170
Mr. Marvin E. Smith, Director

FERGUSON LIBRARY
Public Library of Stamford, Ct.
96 Broad St.
Stamford, Conn. 06901
(203) 325-4354
Mr. Ernest A. DiMattia, Jr., Director

Includes the following on-line libraries:

Turn of River Library
Weed Memorial Library

Florida International University
THE ATHENAEUM
Tamiama Trail
Miami, Fla. 33199
(305) 552-2461
Mr. Howard Cordell, Director

Florida State University
STROZIER LIBRARY
Tallahassee, Fla. 32306
(904) 644-5211
Mr. Charles Miller, Director

FLORIDA STATE LIBRARY SYSTEM
R.A. Gray Building
Tallahassee, Fla. 32304
(904) 487-2651
Mr. Barrett Wilkens, Director

FLINT PUBLIC LIBRARY
0126 E. Kearsley St.
Flint, Mich. 48502
(313) 232-7111
Mr. Rand L. Richardson, Director

FRAMINGHAM PUBLIC LIBRARY
929 Worcester Rd.
Framingham, Mass. 01701
(617) 872-7432
Mr. Charles Flaherty, Assistant Director

FRANKFORT PUBLIC LIBRARY DISTRICT
27 Ash St.
Frankfort, Ill. 60423
(815) 469-2423
Ms. Arlene Santoro, Director

GAIL BORDEN PUBLIC LIBRARY DISTRICT
200 N. Grove Ave.
Elgin, Ill. 60120
(312) 742-2411
Mrs. Edna Holland, Director

GLENCOE PUBLIC LIBRARY
320 Park Ave.
Glencoe, Ill. 60022
(312) 835-5056
Mr. Thomas A. Forte, Director

GLENVIEW PUBLIC LIBRARY
1930 Glenview Rd.

Glenview, Ill. 60025
(312) 724-5200
Mr. Peter Bury, Director

GREENWICH LIBRARY
101 W. Putnam Ave.
Greenwich, Conn. 06830
(203) 622-7900
Mr. Nolan Lushington, Director

GROTON PUBLIC LIBRARY
52 Rte. 117, New Town Rd.
Groton, Conn. 06340
(203) 448-1552
Ms. Gretchen Hammerstein, Director

HAMDEN LIBRARY SYSTEM
Miller Memorial Library
2914 Dixwell Ave.
Hamden, Conn. 06518
(203) 248-7747
Ms. Elizabeth Long, Director

Includes the following on-line libraries:

Cheshire Public Library
Community Library, Hamden
Whitneyville Library
Connecticut State Library, Div. of
    Library Development
North Haven Memorial Library
Mt. Carmel Library

HARVEY PUBLIC LIBRARY
155th St. & Turlington Ave.
Harvey, Ill. 60426
(312) 331-0757
Ms. Edna Davis, Director

Houston, University of
M.D. ANDERSON MEMORIAL LIBRARY
4800 Calhoun Blvd.
Houston, Tex. 77004
(713) 749-4241
Mr. Robert Haynes, Interim Director

Includes the following on-line library:

U. of Texas Health Science Center

HUNTER COLLEGE LIBRARY
City University of New York
695 Park Ave. Room 1007C
New York, N.Y. 10021
(212) 570-5529
Mr. David Lane, Director

LIBRARY
LOS ANGELES COUNTY MUSEUM OF NATURAL HISTORY

HUNTINGTON BEACH PUBLIC LIBRARY
AND INFORMATION CENTER
711 Talbert St.
Huntington Beach, Calif. 92647
(714) 536-5481
Mr. Walter W. Johnson, Director

Includes the following on-line libraries:

Banning Annex Library
Graham Annex Library
Main Street Library

HUNTINGTON PUBLIC LIBRARY
338 Main St.
Huntington, N.Y. 11743
(516) 427-5165
Ms. Arlene Straughn, Director

IDAHO FALLS PUBLIC LIBRARY
457 Broadway
Idaho Falls, Idaho 83401
(208) 592-1450
Ms. Jeanne Goodrich, Director

ILLINOIS STATE LIBRARY
Centennial Building
Springfield, Ill. 62756
(217) 782-2994
Mrs. Kathryn Gesterfield, Director

Illinois, University of
CIRCLE CAMPUS LIBRARY
801 S. Morgan St.
P.O. Box 8198
Chicago, Ill. 60680
(312) 996-2716
Dr. Beverly Lynch, Dean of Libraries

Includes the following on-line library:

Science Library

INDIAN TRAILS PUBLIC LIBRARY DISTRICT
850 Jenkins Court
Wheeling, Ill. 60090
(312) 537-4011
Mr. Kenneth G. Swanson, Director

INDIANAPOLIS-MARION COUNTY
PUBLIC LIBRARY
40 East Saint Clair St.
Indianapolis, Ind. 46204
(317) 635-5662
Mr. Raymond Gnat, Director

Johns Hopkins University
MILTON S. EISENHOWER LIBRARY
Charles & 34th Sts.
Baltimore, Md. 21218
(301) 338-8325
Dr. Richard Polascek, Acting Director

KALAMAZOO PUBLIC LIBRARY
315 South Rose St.
Kalamazoo, Mich. 49007
(616) 342-9837
Dr. Mark Crum, Director

KANSAS CITY PUBLIC LIBRARY
311 East 12th St.
Kansas City, Mo. 64106
(816) 221-0063
Mr. Harold Jenkins, Director

Includes the following on-line libraries:

Northeast Library
Westport Library
Van Horn Library
Southwest Plaza Library
Plaza Library

LAKE FOREST PUBLIC LIBRARY
360 E. Deerpath
Lake Forest, Ill. 60045
(312) 234-0636
Ms. Louise Wells Kasian, Director

LEARNING RESOURCES CENTER — See
Clark County Community College

LEWIS & CLARK LIBRARY
120 S. Last Chance Mall
Helena, Mont. 59601
(406) 442-2380
Mr. John Nichols, Director

LINCOLN LIBRARY
326 S. Seventh St.
Springfield, Ill. 62701
(217) 525-1204
Mr. Robert E. Wagenknecht, Director

LINCOLN TRAIL LIBRARY SYSTEM
1704 W. Interstate Dr.
Champaign, Ill. 61820
(217) 352-0047
Ms. Elaine Albright, Director

LINCOLNWOOD PUBLIC LIBRARY DISTRICT
4100 West Pratt
Lincolnwood, Ill. 60640
(312) 677-5277
Mr. LaDonna Kienizt, Director

LODI PUBLIC LIBRARY
305 W. Pine St.
Lodi, Calif. 95420
(209) 369-6823
Mr. Leonard L. Lachendro, Director

LONG BEACH PUBLIC LIBRARY
111 West Park Ave.
Long Beach, N.Y. 11561
(516) 432-7201
Ms. Sylvia Eisen, Director

M.D. ANDERSON MEMORIAL LIBRARY — See
Houston, University of

MARIN COUNTY FREE LIBRARY
Civic Center Administration Building
San Rafael, Calif. 94903
(415) 479-1100 X 2577
Mr. Bruce Bajema, County Librarian

Includes the following on-line libraries:

Corte Madera Library
Fairfax Library
Sausalito Public Library
Novato Library
Belvedere-Tiburon Library
Civic Center Regional Library
Mill Valley Library

MARTIN LUTHER KING MEMORIAL LIBRARY
The Public Library of the District of Columbia
901 G Street, NW
Washington, D.C. 20001
(202) 727-1101
Dr. Hardy Franklin, Director, D.C. Public Library

Includes the following on-line libraries:

Chevy Chase Library
Georgetown Library
Fort Davis Library
Woodbridge Library

MICHIGAN CITY PUBLIC LIBRARY
100 East 4th St.
Michigan City, Ind. 46360
(219) 879-4561
Mr. Donald A. Daniels, Director

Includes the following on-line library:

Marquette Mall Branch

MID-YORK LIBRARY SYSTEM
1600 Lincoln Ave.
Utica, N.Y. 13502
(315) 735-8328
Mr. Alfred C. Hasemeier, Director

Montréal, Université de
BIBLIOTHEQUE DES SCIENCES,
HUMAINES, ET SOCIALES
C.P. 6128
Succursale A
Montreal, Quebec
Canada H3C 3J7
(514) 343-7646
Mr. Gilles Chaput, Coordinator Services
Informatises

MONTCLAIR FREE PUBLIC LIBRARY
50 South Fullerton Ave.
Montclair, N.J. 07042
(201) 744-0500
Mr. Philip Clark, Director

Includes the following on-line library:

Bellevue Avenue Library

MOUNT PROSPECT PUBLIC LIBRARY
10 South Emerson St.
Mt. Prospect, Ill. 60056
(312) 253-5675
Ms. Mary Jo Hutchings, Director

NAPA CITY-COUNTY LIBRARY
1150 Division St.
Napa, Calif. 94558
(707) 253-4241
Mrs. Winifred Munger, Director

National Aeronautics and Space Administration
LANGLEY RESEARCH CENTER TECHNICAL
LIBRARY
Mail Stop #85
Hampton, Va. 23665
(804) 827-2786
Mr. Phillip Weatherwax, Director

Nevada, University of, Las Vegas
JAMES R. DICKINSON LIBRARY
4505 Maryland Pkwy.
Las Vegas, Nev. 89154

(702) 739-3286
Mr. Harold H.J. Erickson, Director

Nevada, University of, Reno
NOBLE H. GETCHELI LIBRARY
Reno, Nev. 89507
(702) 784-6528
Mr. Harold G. Morehouse, Director

New School for Social Research
RAYMOND FOGELMAN LIBRARY
65 Fifth Ave.
New York, N.Y. 10003
(212) 741-7901
Mr. Michael Markowitz, Librarian

New York University
ELMER HOLMES BOBST LIBRARY
70 Washington Square South
New York, N.Y. 10012
(212) 598-2140
Mr. Carlton Rochell, Dean of Libraries

Includes the following on-line libraries:

Cooper Union for Advancement of Science and
    Art Library
New School for Social Research Library

Newfoundland, Memorial University of
HENRIETTA HARVEY LIBRARY
Elizabeth Ave.
St. John's, Newfoundland
Canada, A1C 5S7
(709) 753-1200
Mr. Theodore Phillips, University Librarian

Includes the following on-line library:

Medical Library

NORTH HAVEN MEMORIAL LIBRARY
17 Elm St.
North Haven, Conn. 06473
(203) 239-5803
Ms. Mary Faust, Acting Director

NORTH SUBURBAN LIBRARY SYSTEM
200 W. Dundee Rd.
Wheeling, Ill. 60090
(312) 459-1300
Mr. Robert McClarren, System Director

Includes the following on-line libraries:

Cook Memorial Public Library District

Ela Area Public Library District
Glencoe Public Library
Indian Trails Public Library District
Lake Forest Public Library
Lincolnwood Public Library
Northbrook Public Library
Schaumburg Public Library
Warren-Newport Public Library District
Wilmette Public Library District
Winnetka Public Library District
Zion-Benton Public Library District

NORTHBROOK PUBLIC LIBRARY
1201 Cedar La.
Northbrook, Ill. 60062
(312) 272-6224
Mrs. Frances J. Bradbury, Director

NORTHEASTERN ILLINOIS UNIVERSITY
LIBRARY
Bryn Mawr at St. Louis Ave.
Chicago, Ill. 60625
(312) 591-4050 X 469
Mr. Melvin George, Director

NORTHLAKE PUBLIC LIBRARY DISTRICT
231 N. Wolf Rd.
Northlake, Ill. 60164
(312) 562-2301
Ms. Ellen Gray, Director

OAK LAWN PUBLIC LIBRARY
9427 Raymond Ave.
Oak Lawn, Ill. 60453
(312) 422-4990
Mr. J. Michael O'Brien, Director

OAK PARK PUBLIC LIBRARY
Scoville Institute
834 Lake St.
Oak Park, Ill. 60301
(312) 383-5030
Ms. Barbara Ballinger, Director

OCEANSIDE PUBLIC LIBRARY
615 Fourth St.
Oceanside, Calif. 92054
(714) 722-3325
Ms. Helen Nelson, Director

OCEANSIDE FREE LIBRARY
Davison Ave.
Oceanside, N.Y. 11572
(516) 766-2360
Mr. Michael Hodgson, Acting Director

Includes the following on-line library:

Long Beach Public Library

PALO ALTO CITY LIBRARY
1213 Newell Rd.
Palo Alto, Calif. 94303
(415) 329-2436
Mrs. June Fleming, Director

PARMLY-BILLINGS LIBRARY
510 N. Broadway
Billings, Mont. 59101
(406) 248-7393
Mr. Robert M. Cookingham, Director

PAWTUCKET PUBLIC LIBRARY AND REGIONAL INFORMATION CENTER
13 Summer St.
Pawtucket, R.I.
(401) 725-3714
Mr. Lawrence Eaton, Director

Pennsylvania, University of
VAN PELT LIBRARY
3410 Walnut St.
Philadelphia, Pa. 19104
(215) 243-7091
Mr. Richard DeGennaro, Director of Libraries

Includes the following on-line libraries

Fine Arts Library
Lippincott Library
Rosengarten Reserve Room

Portland, Library Association of
MULTNOMAH COUNTY LIBRARY
801 SW 10th Ave.
Portland, Ore. 97205
(503) 223-7201
Mr. James H. Burghardt, Librarian

Includes the following on-line libraries:

Midland Library
Hollywood Library
Rockwood Library
Belmont Library
North Portland Library

Portland Public Library
BAXTER LIBRARY
619 Congress St.
Portland, Me. 04101

(207) 773-4761
Mr. Edward Chenevert, Director

PROVIDENCE PUBLIC LIBRARY
150 Empire St.
Providence, R.I. 02903
(401) 521-7722
Ms. Annalee Bundy, Director

Includes the following on-line libraries:

Olneyville Library
Rochambeau Library
Mt. Pleasant Library
Pawtucket Public Library and Regional
    Information Center
Washington Park Library
Knight Memorial Library
Wanskuck Library

Queens College
PAUL KLAPPER LIBRARY
65-30 Kissena Boulevard
Flushing, N.Y. 11367
(212) 520-7256
Mrs. Shoshana Kaufmann, Head of General
    Reader Services

Includes the following on-line libraries:

Art Library
Music Library

UNIVERSITY OF RHODE ISLAND LIBRARY
Kingston, R.I. 02881
(401) 792-2666
Dean George R. Parks, University Librarian

RICHMOND PUBLIC LIBRARY
Civic Center Plaza & MacDonald Ave.
Richmond, Calif. 94804
(415) 234-6632 X 22
Ms. Theodora Johnson, Director

ROCKFORD PUBLIC LIBRARY
215 North Wyman St.
Rockford, Ill. 61101
(815) 965-6731
Mr. Julius Chitwood, Director

ROLLING PRAIRIE LIBRARY
345 W. Eldorado St.
Decatur, Ill. 62522
(217) 429-2586
Mr. Ray Ewick, Director

Includes the following on-line library:

Decatur Public Library

SALT LAKE CITY PUBLIC LIBRARY
209 East 500 St., South
Salt Lake City, Utah 84111
(801) 363-5733
Mr. Dennis Day, Director

Includes the following on-line libraries:

Sprague Library
Chapman Public Library
Rose Park Library

Salt Lake County Library System
WHITMORE LIBRARY
2197 East 7000 South
Salt Lake City, Utah 84121
(801) 943-7614
Mr. Guy Schuurman, Director

Includes the following on-line libraries:

Calvin S. Smith Library
South Jordan Library
East Mill Creek Library
South Salt Lake Library
Kearns Library
Holladay Library
West Jordan Library
Tyler Library
Peterson Library
Granger Library
Magna Library

SAN FRANCISCO PUBLIC LIBRARY
Civic Center
San Francisco, Calif. 94102
(415) 558-4235
Mr. James Reilly, Systems Librarian

SAUSALITO PUBLIC LIBRARY
420 Litho St.
P.O. Drawer C
Sausalito, Calif. 94965
(415) 332-2325
Ms. Patricia A. Shepard, Director

SCHAUMBURG PUBLIC LIBRARY
32 West Library La.
Schaumburg, Ill. 60172
(312) 885-3373
Mr. Michael Madden, Director

Sherbrooke, Université de
BIBLIOTHEQUE GENERALE
Sherbrooke, Quebec
Canada J1K 2R1
(819) 565-5456
Mr. Guy Cloutier, Director

Includes the following on-line libraries:

Bibliotheque de Droit
Bibliotheque des Sciences
Bibliotheque Médicale

SOLANO COUNTY LIBRARY
1150 Kentucky St.
Fairfield, Calif. 94533
(707) 429-6601
Ms. Josephine Becker, County Librarian

Includes the following on-line libraries:

Fairfield-Suison Community Library
Vacaville Public Library
John F. Kennedy Library
Rio Vista Library
Springstowne Library

SOMERVILLE, PUBLIC LIBRARY OF THE CITY OF
Highland Ave. and Walnut St.
Somerville, Mass. 02143
(617) 623-5000
Ms. Thelma Donovan, Acting Director

STERLING HEIGHTS PUBLIC LIBRARY
40285 Dodge Park Rd.
Sterling Heights, Mich. 48078
(313) 979-5060
Ms. Shelagh Klein, Director

SUBURBAN LIBRARY SYSTEM
125 Tower Dr.
Burr Ridge, Ill. 60521
(312) 325-6640
Mr. Lester L. Stoffel, Executive Director

Includes the following on-line libraries:

Alsip-Merrionette Park Library District
Dolton Public Library District
Eisenhower Public Library District
Elmhurst Public Library
Harvey Public Library
Oak Lawn Public Library
Northlake Public Library District

Oak Park Public Library
Park Forest Public Library
Downers Grove Public Library
Elmwood Park Public Library
Frankfort Public Library District
Blue Island Public Library

University of Texas Health Science Center
LIBRARY
7703 Floyd Curl Dr.
San Antonio, Tex. 78284
(512) 696-6271
Dr. David Kronick, Director

Towson State University
ALBERT F. COOK LIBRARY
York Rd.
Baltimore, Md. 21204
(301) 321-2450
Mr. Thomas Strader, Director

Trinity University
CHAPMAN GRADUATE CENTER LIBRARY
715 Stadium Dr.
San Antonio, Tex. 78284
(512) 736-8121
Mr. Robert Houze, Director of Libraries

Includes the following on-line library:

George Storch Memorial Library

TUCSON PUBLIC LIBRARY
111 E. Pennington
P.O. Box 27470
Tucson, Ariz. 85726
(602) 791-4391
Mr. John F. Anderson, Director

Includes the following on-line libraries:

G. Freeman Woods Library
Valencia Public Library
Columbus Library
Himmel Park Library
Wilmot Library

Utah, University of
MARRIOTT LIBRARY
Salt Lake City, Utah 84112
(801) 581-8204
Mr. Roger Hanson, Director

VACAVILLE PUBLIC LIBRARY
680 Merchant St.

Vacaville, Calif. 95688
(707) 448-4900
Mr. Grady Zimmerman, Director

WARREN-NEWPORT PUBLIC LIBRARY DISTRICT
951 North Rt. 21
Gurnee, Ill. 60031
(312) 244-5150
Ms. Carla Funk, Director

WATERFORD PUBLIC LIBRARY
49 Rope Ferry Rd.
Waterford, Conn. 06385
(203) 422-8551
Ms. Patricia Holloway, Director

WASHINGTON, D.C. PUBLIC LIBRARY — See
MARTIN LUTHER KING MEMORIAL LIBRARY

WASHOE COUNTY LIBRARY
301 S. Center St., P.O. Box 2151
Reno, Nev. 89505
(702) 785-4190
Mr. William E. Andrews, Director

WATSONVILLE PUBLIC LIBRARY
310 Union St.
Watsonville, Calif. 95076
(408) 722-2408
Ms. Seely Sumpf, Librarian

Western Michigan University
DWIGHT B. WALDO LIBRARY
Kalamazoo, Mich. 49008
(616) 383-4952
Mr. Carl Sachtleben, Director

Includes the following on-line libraries:

Business Library
Educational Resources Center
Physical Science Library
Music Library

WILMETTE PUBLIC LIBRARY DISTRICT
1242 Wilmette Ave.
Wilmette, Ill. 60091
(312) 256-5025
Richard E. Thompson, Director

WINNETKA PUBLIC LIBRARY DISTRICT
768 Oak St.
Winnetka, Ill. 60093
(312) 446-7220
Ms. Joan Harris, Director

Wisconsin, University of, Oshkosh
FORREST R. POLK LIBRARY
University Libraries and Learning Resources
80 Algoma Blvd.
Oshkosh, Wis. 54901
(414) 424-3333
Ms. Jean Pelletiere, Acting Director

Includes the following on-line libraries:

Learning Resources Center
Halsey Resource Center

YALE UNIVERSITY
120 High St., Box 1603A
Yale Station, Conn. 06520
(203) 436-8335
Mr. Rutherford D. Rogers, University Librarian

Youngstown State University
WILLIAM F. MAAG, JR. LIBRARY
410 Wick Ave.
Youngstown, Ohio 44555
(216) 746-1851 X 431
Ms. Carol Wall, Assistant Librarian for Public Services

ZION-BENTON PUBLIC LIBRARY DISTRICT
2600 Emmaus Ave.
Zion, Ill. 60099
(312) 872-4680
Ms. Jo Ann Ellingson, Director

4. DATAPHASE SYSTEMS, INC.
4528 Belleview
Kansas City, Mo. 64111
(816) 931-7927

WICHITA PUBLIC LIBRARY
223 S. Main St.
Wichita, Kans. 67202
(316) 262-0611
Richard Rademacher, Director
No. of branches: 7
Annual circulation: 450,000
No. of titles: 150,000
No. of items: 250,000
No. of patrons: 65,000
CPU type: Data Gen. NOVA 3/D
No. of terminals: 3
Disk amount: 192 megabyte

TACOMA PUBLIC LIBRARY
1102 Tacoma Ave. So.
Tacoma, Wash. 98402
(206) 572-2000
Kevin Hegarty, Director

No. of branches: 8
Annual circulation: 1,500,000
No. of titles: 250,000
No. of items: 500,000
No. of patrons: 30,000
CPU type: Data Gen. NOVA 3/D
No. of terminals: 20
Disk amount: 600 megabyte

HOUSTON PUBLIC LIBRARY
500 McKinney Ave.
Houston, Tex. 77002
(713) 224-5441
Jay Clark, Chief, Technical Services
No. of branches: 32
Annual circulation: 5,200,000
No. of titles: 300,000
No. of items: 1,875,000
No. of patrons: 600,000
CPU type: Data Gen. ECLIPSE S/130
No. of terminals: 26 initially
Disk amount: 384 megabyte

UNIVERSITY OF NEBRASKA (Dec. 1978)
Lincoln, Neb. 68588
(402) 472-2526
Dr. Brice Hobrock, Asst. Dean
No. of branches: 26
Annual circulation: 5,200,000
No. of titles: 335,000
No. of items: 1,800,000
No. of patrons: 610,000
CPU type: Data Gen. ECLIPSE S/230
No. of terminals: 40
Disk amount: 384 megabyte

ORAL ROBERTS UNIVERSITY
7777 South Lewis
Tulsa, Okla. 74171
(918) 492-6161
Terry Pierce
No. of branches: 3
Annual circulation: 450,000
No. of titles: 300,000
No. of items: 500,000
No. of patrons: 5,000
CPU type: Data Gen. ECLIPSE S/130
No. of terminals: 12
Disk amount: 384 megabyte

DALLAS COUNTY COMMUNITY COLLEGE
DISTRICT
1931 N. Industrial Blvd.
Dallas, Tex. 75207
(214) 746-2260
Paul E. Dumont, Head, Tech. Serv.

No. of branches: 7 campuses & technical
   services
Annual circulation: 250,000
No. of titles: 125,000
No. of items: 200,000
No. of patrons: 50,000
CPU type: Data Gen. NOVA 3/D S/230
No. of terminals: 14
Disk amount: 192 megabyte

ATLANTA PUBLIC LIBRARY (March 1979)
10 Pryor St., S.W.
Atlanta, Ga. 30303
(404) 688-4636
Nancy Eaton, Head, Tech. Serv.
   No. of branches: 28
   Annual circulation: 2,500,000
   No. of titles: 221,000
   No. of items: 1,000,000
   No. of patrons: 230,000
   CPU type: Data Gen. ECLIPSE S/230
   No. of terminals: 60
   Disk amount: 576 megabyte

PUBLIC LIBRARY OF CHARLOTTE &
MECKLENBURG COUNTY (February 1979)
310 N. Tryon St.
Charlotte, N.C. 28202
(704) 374-2530
Arial Stephens, Director
   No. of branches: 16
   Annual circulation: 1,500,000
   No. of titles: 200,000
   No. of items: 600,000
   No. of patrons: 150,000
   CPU type: Data Gen. ECLIPSE S/130
   No. of terminals: 10
   Disk amount: 384 megabyte

GREENSBORO PUBLIC LIBRARY (December 1978)
201 N. Greene St.
Greensboro, N.C. 27402
(919) 373-2474
George Viele, Director
   No. of branches: 8
   Annual circulation: 890,000
   No. of titles: 175,000
   No. of items: 500,000
   No. of patrons: 60,000
   CPU type: Data Gen. ECLIPSE S/130
   No. of terminals: 20
   Disk amount: 384 megabyte

5. DECICOM SYSTEMS, INC.
   250 Adams Blvd.

Farmingdale, N.Y. 11735
(516) 293-9270

EAST MEADOW PUBLIC LIBRARY
Front St. and Newbridge Ave.
East Meadow, N.Y. 11554

HEWLETT-WOODMERE PUBLIC LIBRARY
1125 Broadway
Hewlett, N.Y. 11557

NORTH BELLMORE PUBLIC LIBRARY
1551 Newbridge Ave.
North Bellmore, N.Y. 11710

SHELTER ROCK PUBLIC LIBRARY
165 Searingtown Rd.
Albertson, N.Y. 11507

**6. GAYLORD AUTOMATED CIRCULATION
CONTROL SYSTEM**
Gaylord Library Systems, a division of
Gaylord Bros.
P.O. Box 61
Syracuse, New York 13201
(315) 457-5070

BREVARD COUNTY LIBRARY SYSTEM
1195 N. Courtenay Pkwy.
Merritt Island, Fla. 32952

COMMACK PUBLIC LIBRARY
64 Hauppauge
Commack, N.Y. 11725

FOUNTAINDALE PUBLIC LIBRARY DISTRICT
300 W. Briarcliff Rd.
Bolingbrook, Ill. 60439

LIVERPOOL PUBLIC LIBRARY
Tulip & Second Sts.
Liverpool, N.Y. 13088

LONGVIEW PUBLIC LIBRARY
1600 Louisiana St.
Longview, Wash. 98632

MANHATTAN PUBLIC LIBRARY
Juliette and Poyntz
Manhattan, Kans. 66502

ONONDAGA LIBRARY SYSTEM
355 Montgomery St.
Syracuse, N.Y. 13202

PUBLIC LIBRARY OF COLUMBUS AND
FRANKLIN COUNTY
96 S. Grant St.
Columbus, Ohio 43215

QUEENS BOROUGH PUBLIC LIBRARY
89-11 Merrick Blvd.
Jamaica, N.Y. 11432

UNIVERSITY CITY PUBLIC LIBRARY
6701 Delmar
St. Louis, Mo. 63130

Demonstration site at:
SONOMA COUNTY LIBRARY
Third and E Sts.
Santa Rosa, Calif. 95404

7. INNOVATED SYSTEMS
10920 Indian Trail
Suite 301
Dallas, Tex. 75229
(214) 620-0241

UNIVERSITY OF TEXAS, DALLAS
Dallas, Tex. 75235

8. SCICON
Systems Control, Inc.
1801 Page Mill Rd.
Palo Alto, Calif. 94304
(415) 494-1165

SAN JOSE PUBLIC LIBRARY
180 W. San Carlos St.
San Jose, Calif. 95113

Contract bid awarded at:
MONTGOMERY COUNTY DEPARTMENT OF
PUBLIC LIBRARIES
99 Maryland Ave.
Rockville, Md. 20850

9. ULISYS
Universal Library Systems Ltd.
Suite 202
60 St. Clair Ave. E.
Toronto, Ontario M4T 1N5
Canada
(416) 961-1011

U.S. Installations

PHOENIX PUBLIC LIBRARY
12 E. McDowell Rd.
Phoenix, Ariz. 85004

NORTHLAND PUBLIC LIBRARY
300 Cumberland Rd.
Pittsburgh, Pa. 15237

Canadian Installations

CARIBOO THOMPSON NICOLA LIBRARY SYSTEM
Kamloops, British Columbia
Canada

MINISTRY OF STATE FOR SCIENCE
AND TECHNOLOGY
Ottawa, Canada

Bibliography

Blackwell North America, Inc. *Consultant's Report: Evaluation of Responses to TPL,* May 17, 1977.

"CLSI and Brodart Introduce the LIBS 100/IROS Interface at ALA." *Journal of Library Automation* 10:380 (December 1977).

DeGennaro, Richard. "Doing Business with Vendors in the Computer-Based Library Systems Marketplace." *American Libraries* 9:212+ (April 1978).

"Epic Data Introduces Programmable Collection Units." *Computerworld,* January 31, 1977, p. 34.

Foil, Patti Sue and Bradley D. Carter. "Survey of Data Collection Systems for Computer-Based Library Circulation Processes." *Journal of Library Automation* 9:221-33 (September 1976).

Hegarty, Kevin. *Acquisition of a Computerized Circulation Control System for Tacoma Public Library,* April 1, 1977.

Hegarty, Kevin. *Conversion: The Tacoma Method; a Manual of Procedures. Outline,* January 1978.

Hegarty, Kevin. *Request for Proposals for a Computerized Library Circulation Control System TPL 7603.* Tacoma Public Library, March 23, 1977.

" 'Home Brew' Saves $$ in Georgia." *Library Journal* 102:673 (March 15, 1977).

Markuson, Barbara Evans. "Automated Circulation Control Systems: An Overview of Commercially Available Systems." *Library Technology Reports* (July and September 1975).

LIBRARY
LOS ANGELES COUNTY MUSEUM OF NATURAL HISTORY

Markuson, Barbara Evans. "Granting Amnesty and Other Fascinating Aspects of Automated Circulation." *American Libraries* 9:205-11 (April 1978).

"Mini Helps Library Users Borrow Books." *Computerworld,* May 24, 1976.

"Online Circulation: Costs Pegged." *Library Journal* 102:33 (April 15, 1977).

Scholz, William. "Computer-based Circulation Systems — A Current Review and Evaluation." *Library Technology Reports* 13:231-326 (May 1977).

Stiefel, Mal. "Library 'Checks Out' Inventory with OCR Wands Linked to CPU." *Computerworld,* January 24, 1977.

"The Age of Miracle Chips." *Time* 111:44, 45 (February 20, 1978).

Thorson, A. Robert. "The Economics of Automated Circulation." In *The Economics of Library Automation.* Ed. J.L. Divilbiss (Clinic on Library Applications of Data Processing, 13th). Urbana-Champaign, Illinois: University of Illinois, Graduate School of Library Science, 1977, pp. 28-47.

Index

American Library Association 1, 30, 38
American National Standards Institute 77
American University 9, 13, 45
Anaheim Public Library 61
Arizona Public Library 69
Arlington County Public Libraries 9
Automated Library Systems, Ltd. 2, 72
Azurdata 52

Baker & Taylor 7, 82, 86
Baldwin Public Library 45
BALLOTS 7, 65-66, 82, 86
Bear Ridge Suburban Library System 40
Blackwell North America, Inc. 13, 19, 20, 23,
    50, 81
BLOCS I & II 2
Blue Island Public Library 16
British Columbia, University of 45
Brodart 7, 37, 39, 81, 82
Bucknell University 2, 8

Check-a-Book 9
Checkpoint/Mark II Book Theft Detection
    System 14
Checkpoint/Plessey 1, 7, 10, 13, 24-29, 74, 75
Checkpoint Systems, Inc. 9, 70
Chicago, University of 8-9, 29-30
Cincinnati Electronics 1, 9, 10, 12, 14, 29-36,
    64, 74, 79, 80
CIRC 7, 72-73, 81
Circulation systems, automated (see also
    individual systems)
  absence 10, 16
  batch processing, 6, 10
  call number vs. access number 11-12
  conversion 12-14
  costs 6, 8, 15-16, 17, 85
  criteria for acquisition 18-23
  home-grown 2, 7-9, 16-17
  impetus for 6-7, 84-86
  implications 79-83
  inventory 10-11
  literature 18-19
  OCR vs. bar-coded labels 12
  on-line vs. off-line 11
  packaged 9-10
  reasons against 5-6, 85
  study conclusions 3-4
  systems 24-73
  users' comments 74-78
Clark Co. District Library 82
CLASSIC see Cincinnati Electronics
CL Systems, Inc. (CLSI) 1, 5, 6, 9, 10, 12, 13,
    15, 16, 19, 21, 22, 23, 36-46, 64, 74, 76,
    79, 80, 81, 82, 85
Columbus & Franklin Co. Public Library 54
Commack Public Library 6, 14, 84

Dallas Community College District 7, 14, 15, 21
DataPhase 1, 7, 10, 12, 13, 14, 19, 23, 46-51,
    74, 77, 81-82, 85
Data General Corp. 47, 51
Decicom Systems, Inc. 1, 23, 51-53, 74, 77
Digital Equipment Corp. 39, 55-56, 60, 62, 66,
    67, 69

East Brunswick Public Library 2, 8, 17, 86
East Meadow Public Library 52
Electronic security system connections 14-15
ENIAC 3
Epic Data 2, 3, 13, 45

Fairfax Co. Public Library 19, 22
Florida State University System 82

Gaylord Bros., Inc. 1, 6, 7, 10, 11, 13, 14, 23,
    53-61, 73, 74, 77, 80, 85
Greensboro Public Library 6, 18, 22

Harvey Public Library 16, 22
Henrico Co. Library System 30, 74
Hewlett-Packard 71
Hewlett-Woodmere Public Library 52
Honeywell 2

IBM 2, 6, 7, 8, 9, 15
ICC/Plessey 10, 12, 23, 70-71, 74
Illinois, University of 8, 86

Innovated Systems 14, 37, 64, 71-72, 80
International Computing 9, 70
IROS 37, 39, 81

Kansas City Public Library 82
Kentucky Center for Energy Research 30, 74, 79
Knogo Corp. 2, 14, 72

Lear-Siegler 62
Lewis & Clark Library 16
Library Control System 8, 86
Library Services Construction Act 18
LIBS 100 see CL Systems, Inc.
Liverpool Public Library 53
Lockheed 86

3M Co. 9, 14, 19, 71
Macon/Bibb Co. Public Library 8
Manhattan Public Library 13
Milwaukee Co. Federated Library System 25
Mitre Corp. 19, 83
Mohawk Data 9
Monarch 8, 62, 67, 70
Montclair Free Public Library 45
Montgomery Co. Dept. of Public Libraries 61

Nassau Library System 52
National SemiConductor 52
NCR 8
Nevada, University of 82
New York, State University of 8
New York University 16, 45, 81, 84
North Bellmore Public Library 52
North Carolina State Library System 46
North Carolina State University 30
Northland Public Library 7, 11, 13, 15, 20-21, 66, 78, 82
North Suburban Library System 41, 82

OCLC 13-14, 62, 65-66, 73, 81
Ohio State University 8, 15, 86
Oklahoma City Library 8
Onondaga County Libraries 55

Pennsylvania, University of 6, 9, 13, 45
Phoenix Public Library 3, 13, 68, 70, 78
Pittsburgh, University of 8
Plessey Telecommunications 9, 70
Princeton University 9

Recognition Products, Inc. 8
Resource pooling 80-81

Salt Lake City Co. Library 40
San Jose Public Library 13, 14, 15, 20, 61-62, 78, 81
SCICON see Systems Control, Inc.
Shelter Rock Public Library 52
South Carolina, University of 5
Sperry Univac 30, 35, 36
Standard Register 7
Suburban Library System 15, 41, 80, 82
Syracuse University 8
Systems Control, Inc. 1, 10, 12, 13, 14, 15, 19, 23, 61-66, 70, 74, 78, 81, 82, 85

Tacoma Public Library 12, 13, 19-21, 23, 50-51, 77, 81, 86
Technology, new 79-80
Texas Medical Center 30
Texas, University of (Dallas) 14, 37, 71-72
Texas, University of (Permian Basin) 25
Toronto, University of Library 2, 73
TPS Electronics 14, 62
Tucson Public Library 6, 40

UCLA 14
ULYSIS see Universal Library Systems, Inc.
Universal Library Systems, Inc. 1, 3, 7, 10, 11, 12, 13, 23, 63, 66-70, 74, 78, 80, 82
University of Toronto Library Automation System (UTLAS) 2, 72, 81
U.S. Air Force Academy 25

Villanova University 25
Visits, on-site 21

Washington Library Network 19, 50, 81
Winnipeg, University of 66
Wisconsin, University of 45

ABOUT THE AUTHOR

Alice Harrison Bahr is the author of *Book Theft and Library Security Systems, 1978-79* and *Microforms: The Librarians' View, 1978-79* in the Professional Librarian Series. A graduate of Temple University, she holds an M.L.S. from Drexel University and an M.A. and Ph.D. from Lehigh University. From 1971 to 1974 she was Assistant Reference Librarian and Acting Government Documents Librarian at Lehigh. She currently teaches at Cedar Crest College and is a freelance researcher and writer on a wide variety of subjects.